This book provides the mindshift necessary to get ahead and start in the Australian Property market. Well written and informative, the book cuts through the jargon of the investment world and provides the reader with all the information required to go out and start their own investing career. Financial stress is the leading cause of stress in Australia and this book provides the information to dispel all the fear associated with getting ahead in the property market.

- Dylan Conway Founder of Brothers and Books LTD

=============

A practical, well-written and thought-provoking book that has changed the way I now view certain aspects of the property market.

-Alex Gerrick, Author, A Season of Clouds

=============

Shortcut to Freedom is an easy to read analysis of property investing in Australia. The author is well-researched. We recommend this book to anyone just starting out in property investment or looking to build a property portfolio. With the suggestions plus timing, an investor is well guided to succeed with a long term property portfolio.

-Phillip J Anderson, author of The Secret Life of Real Estate and Banking and the Property Share market Economics team.

SHORTCUT TO FREEDOM

MAKING MILLIONS THROUGH PROPERTY INVESTMENT

JACOB CAMILLERI

Disclaimer: The information in this publication and the links provided are for general information only and should not be taken as constituting professional financial advice from the author or publisher.

Jacob Camilleri is not a financial adviser. You should consider seeking independent legal, financial, taxation or other advice to check how the website information relates to your unique circumstances.

Jacob Camilleri, Ocean Reeve Publishing or any endorsers of this publication are not liable for any loss caused, whether due to negligence or otherwise arising from the use of, or reliance on, the information provided directly or indirectly, by information provided in this publication.

Shortcut to Freedom: Making Millions Through Property Investment

Edited by Evan Hanford

ISBN: 978-1-923061-17-0 (paperback)

NATIONAL LIBRARY OF AUSTRALIA

A catalogue record for this book is available from the National Library of Australia

Printed in Australia by Ocean Reeve Publishing
www.oceanreevepublishing.com
Published by Jacob Camilleri and Ocean Reeve Publishing

Ocean REEVE PUBLISHING

CONTENTS

1

THE JSC WAY

Don't invest in real estate. It's too risky, prices are too high, you have to deal with tenants and they will break your stuff! Prices will plummet, the bubble will burst, and you'll be paying the loan back for the rest of your life. Your property will sit vacant with no income, it will be hard to sell if you need to, all the while paying for its upkeep in maintenance. The whole thing is fraught with danger.

Excited yet? I know I am.

These are the typical responses I get when talking to most people about property investing. And that's great! More real estate for the rest of us.

For most people, problems are problems, and they lead to excuses and resistance.

But for people like Simon (my brother and business partner) and I, and people who read real estate books to expand their knowledge and are open to learning new ideas, obstacles can lead to opportunity.

And what an opportunity we have here, at our fingertips.

I want to take you back to 2014. The year 'Let it Go' dominated the charts – that's right, it was about a decade ago.

I was twenty years old, and being ever the optimist (thanks, Mum), I knew there must be a way to live the life I wanted and not be stuck for forty odd years in a job that brought no sense of fulfillment, no sense of self-worth. I had a great income, savings, and extremely limited financial liabilities. On paper, I was doing exceptionally well for my age. But is that what was life is all about?

It was a difficult predicament, with drive and motivation but nowhere to direct it, to focus this energy. I felt as though time was being wasted, like being behind the wheel of a Lamborghini on a race track with a speed limiter. It just didn't feel right.

Until one day the planets aligned and I found the very thing that would give me my freedom. A family member handed me a property investing book, which immediately sparked my interest. Thankfully the author was one of the good ones: genuine, authentic, dismissive of hidden commissions and agendas. This is hard to come by in a largely unregulated industry.

I have my brother-in-law, Sam Thorpe, to thank for this, the most dedicated Air Force veteran and loyal human being I've ever known.

The author kept it simple, and the premise was easy to understand. Buy the right investment property and it will grow in value, rents will increase, but the mortgage will stay the same (or reduce). All you need to do is manage this debt, ensure the rental income covers most or all of the repayments, and in time its worth will snowball far beyond what most incomes could possibly achieve.

It was my way out. I envisioned living a life on my own terms.

What if I could actually sleep in whenever I'm sick?

What if I don't have to get critiqued on my job performance like a petulant child?

What if I could afford to work a low-paying job that I enjoy, whilst still growing significantly wealthier as time goes on?

What if I didn't have to answer to anyone?

All these ideas and more started emerging in my head, like a garden bursting into life.

Imagine the first moment of this discovery in a person's life.

You can be free.

And I'm going to help you.

From that moment on, the addiction began. Property books became my drug of choice, and I found myself buying every single one I could find. Google was having a field day throwing about property investment book recommendations on every site imaginable. Every time I was bored on the computer, the search engine always knew how to lead me down the rabbit hole to that dopamine hit of a new property book.

As an impressionable, inexperienced, and naïve young man, it was nothing short of a God-given miracle that I didn't go ahead with the purchase of a number of what I would now describe as 'portfolio-crippling properties'. These properties were offered to me by several different property sourcing specialists and marketers. Thinking back, one of them was essentially an oversized shoe-box in outback Queensland, a part of a large complex of identical mediocre units. It wasn't even built yet.

I remember the price of that one was about $300,000.

By the end of this book, you'll have absolute clarity on why a property like this has no place in a successful portfolio.

I don't remember why I chose not to sign the dotted line on each occasion. But I was approached on many occasions by pushy property spruikers talking up high rental returns, tax-saving benefits, stamp duty savings, and low deposits.

They never mentioned I would have to pay $50,000 - $100,000 more than what the property was actually worth, and that the value of a property's location is the true driver of its growth over time.

Maybe this younger Jacob wasn't as naïve as I thought.

Unfortunately, young Jacob still made mistakes. But I have no regrets, because wisdom is born of mistakes, and experience is the ultimate teacher.

A decade of endlessly reading, researching, and active investing has led me to today. Over that period, I've made countless mistakes and had many successes.

I was lucky enough to work as a buyer's agent for another company who noticed my passion and knowledge and offered me the role. This was the first time I could use my experience on a professional level, and I quickly realised how exceptionally beneficial a great buyer's agent service was to an inexperienced investor.

My passion and work life were finally synced, and my employers were fair, intelligent, and had exceptional leadership skills.

And great leadership is an art form, rare as diamonds in the world of real estate today.

But that's another story.

Property investing had never really been a common topic of conversation among my peers before this time, and it's probably the same story for you. Have you ever tried broaching the subject with family or friends?

Most people have made their minds up when it comes to the topic, and, like a pistol in the holster, the vast majority have no shortage of excuses at the ready. Considering that typical human behaviour is to become ever-more entrenched in our preconceived opinions, it can be challenging to find support among those closest to us.

It takes a far more developed and advanced mind to be receptive to new ideas.

To accept that what we think we know could be wrong.

At times, I felt like the black sheep in the crowd, and you might have felt this way too. Property investing can at times be a lonely road. Especially after purchasing three to four properties - it's just not popular.

Perhaps it's the Tall Poppy Syndrome, perhaps it's the fact that less than 0.7% of the Australian population own three or more properties (according to the ATO – for the 2019/2020 financial year). And people tend to follow the crowd.

I never had a doubt that I was going down the right path. I kept my faith and never lost sight of my dream.

I refused to be paralysed by indecision. Refused to question everything I'd achieved.

I kept moving forward.

And it's been exceptionally rewarding.

I guess Henry Ford was right when he said that "Whether you think you can or think you can't, you're right."

The purpose of this book is to save you years of time and energy, not to mention money, by bringing forward your tangible results and rewards from successful investing. Not only through choosing the highest-performing property investments, but also by avoiding significant financial loss by following the wrong guidance.

One mistake can set your journey and your freedom back by many years.

This book will save you from wasting enormous sums of money on the wrong properties and teach you how to get the best possible price on the right properties.

It will even save you countless hours of researching complex and unnecessary property investment strategies that only yield worse results.

It will also save you from moving forward with the wrong advice, the wrong mentor, and a life of financial stress and worry.

At the very least, you will learn:

- How to avoid losing hundreds of thousands in unnecessary commissions
- How to begin your portfolio for maximum cash flow benefit whilst not sacrificing any growth potential
- How to decide on which city and suburb to buy in
- How to select the right property in that suburb
- How to save tens of thousands on every property purchase

- Peace-of-mind over your property and mortgage
- How to reach financial freedom many years sooner, and
- The unfair advantage that a great buyer's agent brings to the table.

Equipped with the right knowledge and the proper team, you will outperform other investors, capitalise more effectively on the booms, and weather the recession storms far better than everyone else.

Your results will be unique to you, because every suburb in every city will perform slightly differently. Most properties in the same suburb will have their own nuisances and characteristics, affecting the overall investment.

Even your loan will have certain features and rates that others won't.

Your team along the way will impact your results greatly – the right buyer's agent, the right mortgage broker, and the right property manager will streamline your real-time results and take the stress out of the whole process.

So, in a largely unregulated industry, with spruikers and scammers on every corner, how is someone new to this real-life Monopoly game supposed to know who the right team is for them? Or even where to look?

It was with that purpose that JSC Property Investments was founded. We imagine a world where anyone willing to take the plunge into property investing can easily find genuine guidance, without the fear of hidden agendas, wasted time, or ending up with a poor property investment.

We'll forever remain unbiased on properties recommended to clients, and any developers or spruikers who approach us offering referral fees to push their stock to our clients won't ever get their foot in the door.

Unfortunately, not all companies turn these offers away. Many agencies are set on new builds, buying off-the-plan, house and land packages, or charge nothing to pennies for their services. This is a tell-tale sign that there are very likely background commissions being paid. And where do these commissions come from? Someone has to pay them. This is where the ambiguously high purchase price comes into play – the commission is simply added on top.

It's your money, so why don't they have your best interests at heart?

2

CONFINES OF THE 9-5

This book is designed to prove to you that you can create a low-risk, high performing property portfolio that will effectively and efficiently grow your wealth, replace your income, and give you the choices in life that very few people will ever attain.

Your time is limited, and your time is valuable. With only twenty-four hours in a day, we can only trade so much of our time for money. Even with a great career and a modestly rising salary, the model is entirely based on time spent at work.

Do you love your job?

Are you happy and warm?

Do you sleep well at night?

Would you continue in the same job if you made $100,000 per year regardless if you showed up or not?

How we spend our days is how we spend our lives, so if you believe that changes need to be made, or you just want some extra financial security and passive income for the ride, then real estate may just be the answer.

Currently in Australia in 2023, someone on $60,000 per annum will take home $48,833 after tax. Someone on $120,000 will take home $88,133. The difference in salary is $60,000, but the difference in after-tax dollars is only $39,300. The way tax brackets are designed in Australia is to create a more even result between a higher income and a lower income earner by taxing accordingly. This model proves that by putting in more hours and working more overtime, or taking on more jobs and responsibilities to increase your day-job income, the higher you will be taxed, and therefore a lower value will be assigned to time spent working.

Chasing a higher and higher salary in a job you don't enjoy will decrease your life satisfaction, while not being equally rewarded for your time and effort as you move up the designated tax brackets.

But there is a solution.

If you don't like where you are, change it. You are not a tree. – The late Jim Rohn

3

TIME IS YOUR ADVANTAGE

Time is an investor's friend. In time, poor property investments can turn out alright, just as a great property investment can turn into a cash machine. With, say, four investment properties, you have access to the growth over time of four markets, which, if done right, can earn you far more than an entire year of income from working.

With the passage of time, inflation will chip away at your mortgage, even if you choose not to pay it down. Additionally, Australia will be richer and busier, and well-located land will become ever more valuable. You won't need to save or budget or worry about bills at all as your property does the heavy lifting for you. Compound interest will snowball, and your net worth will propel you far beyond the limitations of a day job.

Time is also a tremendous reason to buy when there is negativity in the market, and in the economy. Think back to all property downturns you've ever lived through. Wouldn't they have been exceptional times to buy well-located investment-grade properties?

Residential property in Australia has a tendency to boom when exiting a period of contraction, once the crowd is comfortable to enter the market once again. However, the biggest profits have been made by those who took the plunge when the crowd was on stand-by, that is to say those who invested knowing that Australia would bounce back and prosper once again.

Life is a cycle of ups and downs; the good times and bad times are evanescent, so why not make the most of both sentiments? See the opportunity for what it is, and use time to your advantage.

4

THE GREAT MINDSET SHIFT

One of the biggest traditional mindsets about debt is focusing on how much interest you will pay the bank over the life of the loan, rather than focusing on your overall cash flow position.

It's easy to find out how much interest you will pay over the life of the loan, and there are many of these online calculators available. You can manipulate the figures to reflect extra repayments, and the 'total interest paid' figure reduces. Obviously, you should focus your efforts on buying one property and completely paying it off, right?

Incorrect.

Yes, you will save a lot on interest.

But at a severe opportunity cost.

It may take fifteen to twenty years of extra repayments to pay this loan off, and you may have saved $200,000 in interest over that period. Now, imagine a second investment property compounding over that time instead. The property that could have been bought for $600,000, renting at $500 per week is now worth $1,500,000, renting at $850 per week (conservative growth figures).

The lesson here: let leverage and compound growth do the work for you.

Think about the habits of the rich. Specifically, the self-made rich, those who have become financially free well before retirement age. The ones who weren't born into wealth and now don't have to ever work again if they so choose. What percentage of them do you think became financially free through purely saving their income and letting it sit in a savings account or term deposit, nothing more, nothing less?

I'm happy to have a crack at a guess. One per cent?

The vast majority probably started or bought a business or two, bought real estate, got educated about the share market, or found their specific niche in the marketplace, and ran with it.

Do you think any of them would say that they worked nine to five and saved their way to financial freedom? I wonder how they spent their weekends the past thirty years?

The limitations of time and tax means that the theory that you can save your way to wealth is greatly flawed (on most Australian incomes anyway). Just as inflation assists investors by reducing the intrinsic value of their mortgage debt, it is the enemy of the saver as the value of their cash savings diminishes year after year.

I'm starting to think that doing nothing with your money is riskier.

5

LEVERAGE

The definition of leverage is: *the exertion of force by means of a lever.*

But perhaps more relevant to real estate is the second definition: *use (something) to maximum advantage.*

That something is our deposit. The ability to take $100,000 (an arbitrary figure) to buy a $500,000 investment means you are using the deposit to maximum advantage. The result? Ten per cent growth of a $500,000 property is $50,000. Ten per cent growth of $100,000 in a bank account in $10,000. Compare the pair. Same age, same income. Same financial contribution.

Let's not forget that the $50,000 growth in the property is untaxed gains if you don't sell.

That's a fifty per cent return-on-investment.

Without the power of leverage, saving money will result in a steady, easy-to-predict increase over time and not the exponential growth necessary for significant wealth-creation. As our (investment-grade, carefully selected) assets grow in value and rents increase over time, the snowball gathers momentum and accelerates our wealth-building far beyond the financial limitations of a nine to five existence.

So, while the saver is sticking only to their savings account, collecting six per cent (give or take) interest on their money, their $100,000 investment has grown potentially $4,000 (after tax) without them having to work.

Actually, inflation will erode this even further.

6

COMPOUND GROWTH IN ALL ITS WONDER

Compound growth, or the snowball effect. This is where real estate really gets exciting.

The value of a single high-performing investment property will snowball. As it grows, rental revenue will increase, which will feed back into its growth, which means that you will have more financial capacity and the mortgage will reduce in real dollars (due to inflation) whether you pay it down or not.

Now, apply this concept to three high-performing investment properties. Your money is now working harder than you! What chance does your day job have of keeping up with this momentum?

As a property increases in value, this increases the equity, which is very commonly used to act as a deposit for another property but can be used for a range of purposes by the canny investor. Equity is simply calculated by taking the property's market value and subtracting the mortgage on that property.

If there is enough equity available in your property, mortgage lenders look favourably towards this as a potential deposit for future investments.

With one property, it may take a few years to grow enough to fully fund the next property. With three properties, it may only take twelve months to fund the next. The snowball has grown, and we've entered a higher level of financial ability, one which is sustainable and sets the foundation for the future.

An investor today is able to start with a single house deposit, to carefully select the right property to invest in, and leverage this into a multi-property portfolio compounding over time and eventually replacing their day job.

No requirement to save a deposit every time

Let's compare a scenario where someone saves a modest $30,000 per annum over thirty years, with someone who purchases two well-located investment properties over the same time frame. Setting aside the painful thirty years of budgeting, saving, scrimping, and cutting back, let's simply look at the numbers and the resulting financial position.

- Assumed long-term growth rate: seven point five per cent per annum.

- Assumed long-term rental growth rate: three per cent per annum.
- Two properties purchased.
- Loans on Interest-Only repayments (loans remaining the same amount and not being actively paid down) with no extra repayments ever made over the thirty years.

Scenario 1

Thirty years of saving $30,000 per year = $900,000. With varying savings account returns over time, perhaps this final figure ends up at $2,000,000.

Scenario 2

This involves having saved a deposit for a house after three years ($30,000 x 3 years = $90,000) then buying a well-located investment property for $500,000 (property 1). Several years later, and zero cash saving and budgeting along the way, the growth of the first property fully funds the next investment property (property 2). This investment property is worth $500,000. For this example, let's say both properties began renting out at $450 per week.

At the thirtieth year, using the average long-term growth rates, property 1 is projected to be worth around $3.5 million. Property 2 may have had approximately twenty-two years in the market, and is now projected to be worth around $2.45m. That's a total asset base of $5.95m, with $1,862 combined rental income each week.

As we didn't pay down the debt at all, subtracting the mortgages from the total property values gives us about $5m in equity. Not bad for only saving one deposit!

7
STRATEGIES

There are many strategies successful investors use to build their portfolios. It really comes down to how active you want to be, how much time you have available for your investing, your risk tolerance, and available finance. Some common strategies include:

- buy and hold
- buy, renovate, sell
- subdivide/develop
- negative gearing
- positive gearing.

Positive and negative gearing are resulting financial positions rather than an entire strategy. But an investor absolutely needs to know what they are both about.

Buy and hold

The ever-popular buy and hold strategy. It's popular for good reason in that it has stood the test of time and brought financial freedom to many investors. If the properties you buy to hold are investment-grade, then this strategy will be greatly rewarding.

Many investors like to carry out low-risk cosmetic renovations along the way, which can provide a great short-term equity boost and even bring in a higher rental return.

With buying and selling costs as high as they are today, the less buying and selling you have to do the better.

Here are some estimates of these costs for a $500,000 property, here in 2023. Note that they vary between States and Territories.

Buying

- Stamp Duty: Approx $18,000 (NSW)
- Bank fees: Approx $3,000
- Conveyancing/Solicitor cost for the transfer: $900 - $3,000
- Inspections: $400 - $2,000 as needed

- Lenders Mortgage Insurance (LMI) if loan required is over eighty per cent of the purchase price: $1 - $20,000 (See Chapter 9, Mortgage (LMI graph) for a more accurate estimation of LMI)
- And any potential buyers agent fees

Selling

- Agent selling commission: $10,000 - $20,000 (don't skip this step if you want the highest sale price!)
- Bank fees: Approx $3,000 + any extra early repayment charges
- Conveyancing/Solicitor cost for the transfer: $900 - $3,000
- Capital Gains Tax (CGT): A tax on the sale price if it is higher than what you paid for it. See the ATO website for the most up-to-date information of CGT.

Other fees and charges can rear their ugly heads from time to time. Maybe there's an issue with the title that the solicitor needs to sort out, or maybe the loan application gets delayed and some late settlement fees are charged.

With the best team in your corner, these problems are picked up early and get sorted out efficiently.

Implementing a buy and hold strategy is becoming more and more effective as the transfer costs continue to increase over time.

Buy, renovate, sell

Buy low, sell high – sounds simple, doesn't it?

Yes, when it comes to other investment classes. Not so for real estate!

By global standards, Australia has quite a high taxation system. Combining this with property transfer costs and current capital gains tax legislation means that most investors will fail to turn a profit after a buy, renovate, and sell venture.

Weighing up the risks involved, for most of us it's just not worth it.

For highly experienced renovators looking to add bedrooms, make structural changes, or completely overhaul an ugly duckling, then there is potential for profit to be made.

The purpose of this book isn't to encourage high risk investing to the inexperienced. If you aren't well versed with flipping property and major renovations, don't think you're missing out on enormous lump-sum profits every other month by renovating to sell. It's actually an easy way for inexperienced renovators to go bankrupt.

Subdivide/develop

Another common strategy is to buy a property on a good sized block, subdivide it, then hold or even sell one of the blocks for a lump-sum gain. This is best carried out in a rising market, because subdivision costs are high and there are many roadblocks along the way.

I personally like to buy properties with subdivision potential as they are an extra desirable factor down the track, and this extra potential will be factored in to the overall value of the property. It also means you probably have one of the larger blocks in the area, which is also a level of uniqueness setting your property apart.

Developing essentially means to build a new dwelling. This may involve demolishing the existing dwelling or simply buying a vacant block to build on. The zoning of the land is crucial for developing or subdividing, and this can easily be checked on the local council's website. You are unlikely to be approved to build a completely different structure to those in the surrounding area – such as a high-rise unit block in a low-density residential area, or a house + granny flat where no other properties in the area have previously been allowed to do so.

Developing property has high upfront costs but can be greatly rewarding. Considering that all this cost doesn't give us access to multiple rising markets, we would usually consider such a venture towards the end of a property portfolio rather than the earlier stages.

Negative gearing

Negative gearing is one of the most divisive and misunderstood concepts in real estate.

Essentially, it is a situation where the holding costs of a property (property management, council rates, insurance, maintenance, mortgage etc.) are higher than the income it produces. This results in a net loss to the investor, which the Australian Taxation Office currently allows to offset against the investor's personal income tax.

Without the ability to offset this loss, you would be using after-tax dollars to service your investment, just as you would for an owner-occupied home.

For many properties, cash flow will plummet, and real estate as an investment will not look favourable when compared to returns in other asset classes.

And Australia is already in a perpetual shortage of rental accommodation.

Negative gearing is seen by some people as a shady tax avoidance scheme used by cunning investors to dodge paying their fair share of tax. It's a flawed opinion, and is a good example of the type of misinformation pertaining to property investment today.

However, using negative gearing to save on tax will greatly reduce your ability to grow your portfolio and potentially put you in a high-risk situation.

Unless lending restrictions are greatly eased over time, a significant net loss will not provide an incentive for a lender to approve you for another mortgage. This means that investors in a better cash flow position can continue growing the portfolio and reaching their goals, while the negative geared portfolio reaches its ceiling until income is improved.

A significant net loss could put a strain on the investor's everyday life, increasing to the potential pressure if the property sits vacant, if maintenance problems arise, if the investor loses their job, or if interest rates were to rise.

After a dozen or so RBA interest rate hikes seen across Australia in 2022 and 2023, the potential for finding an investment-grade property and having the property fully pay for itself while holding all costs associated are extremely slim. This means that most properties will be negatively geared initially, and those that aren't may not provide the high growth required in the portfolio. Thankfully, people like you will know how to minimise the expenses and maximise your income to get a better result than the rest of the crowd.

Negative gearing isn't one-size-fits-all. Purchasing a $2,000,000 property might result in a $150,000 annual net loss. A $500,000 property might result in a $5,000 annual net loss. The more expensive property may need over ten years to turn positive, while the more affordable property might only need a couple of years.

The hope for a significant negative gearing endeavour is that the more expensive property will grow more in value than a more affordable property, and the even stronger hope that the market doesn't fall into recession.

Risk and hope seem to be recurring factors at play with negative gearing.

Property cycle timing is far more critical for high-risk negative gearing. If you do decide to go down this path then you will need to buy in the earlier stages of the growth cycle, because value-decline will be far more destructive to your financial situation than otherwise would be.

Through smart buying and ensuring your portfolio is providing solid cash flow, without sacrifice to capital growth, you can remove much of the risk and hope associated with negative gearing.

Positive gearing

On the flip-side of negative gearing we have positive gearing. This is where the income of a property completely covers all holding costs, including the mortgage repayments.

What a comfortable situation to be in.

Does this mean we should all get tunnel-vision on positive gearing and make it wholly and solely the goal of a portfolio?

Of course not.

Cash flow is beneficial, but capital growth is life-changing. Focusing only on cash flow can be extremely limiting to wealth-creation.

Let's say an investor takes positive gearing to the extreme and target small community towns where the prices are low and rents are high. She buys 5 x $200,000 properties that each rent out for approximately $350 per week. She estimates each property will be positive geared $10,000 per year after all expenses.

This results in a $50,000 profit every year.

But what's wrong in this equation? Seems fairly profitable, even close to some degree of financial freedom.

The scenario:

In a given year, one of these properties will need a new air conditioning system, another needs a hot water system, and another might need a termite treatment. Minus $10,000 for that year.

Property management fees are higher than average, because the properties are in remote locations - there aren't the options available for competitive pricing. Minus an extra $2,000 per property every year.

Insurance costs are higher due to higher estimated rebuild costs. Minus an extra $500 per property per year.

Larger deposits will be required because the lender considers the location higher-risk. They also charge a higher interest rate to make up for the added risk. Minus an extra $15,000 per property in deposits upfront and $2,500 per property every year for the higher interest charge.

All maintenance costs are higher, as there just isn't the competition in the area and the investor doesn't have much choice for quotes. Minus an extra $1,500 per property every year.

The profit has vanished, and the properties have had minimal capital or rental growth.

Time, money, and effort has been wasted.

Prolonging the decision to start again will only result in frustration and a feeling of being burned-out. Yet selling up and starting again might leave you worse-off than when you started (with the high buying and selling costs involved).

All these extra charges and headaches can be avoided with smart buying. An investment-grade property starting in the negative will eventually become positive geared. Location is crucial and the numbers alone just don't tell the full story.

What's JSC Property Investments' preferred strategy?

We stick to a strategy that we have both implemented in our own portfolios and have helped many people achieve in theirs.

The strategy is a combination of capital growth plus cash flow properties, potentially with some cosmetic renovation potential, buying into rising or undervalued markets with exceptional long-term growth. The end goal is substantial positive gearing, with a solid growth asset base. Capital growth ensures the portfolio charges forward, while the high rental returns assist with debt, allowing for further borrowing if required, and helping to create freedom and choices in our everyday lives.

Some lesser-known benefits of investment-grade properties we target:

- These properties will be well-located and in strong demand by a range of buyers and tenants decades into the future;
- They will have less vacancy, be easier to sell if required, will attract quality tenants and

tenants who will be able to afford rental increases in-line with market levels;

- They will likely grow on a long-term trend of seven to nine per cent compounding growth per annum with untaxed capital growth, creating the ability to leverage into more assets far sooner than our cashflow strategy example. Rents will also rise at a faster rate;
- Banks and lending institutions will be more willing to lend against a property that is in a large, diverse economy, safe from the volatile fluctuations of small or single-industry towns. This will result in a lower interest rate as they see the mortgage safely secured with low-risk properties. This will also ensure that our borrowing capacity is not unnecessarily limited due to higher-risk locations;

Hopefully it is becoming clearer that there is much more to buying the right property than the numbers alone. Ideally, we want the journey to be a little boring! No hidden surprises along the way.

Below are the historical trends between a typical cash flow property and capital-growth focused property, and how they perform over time:

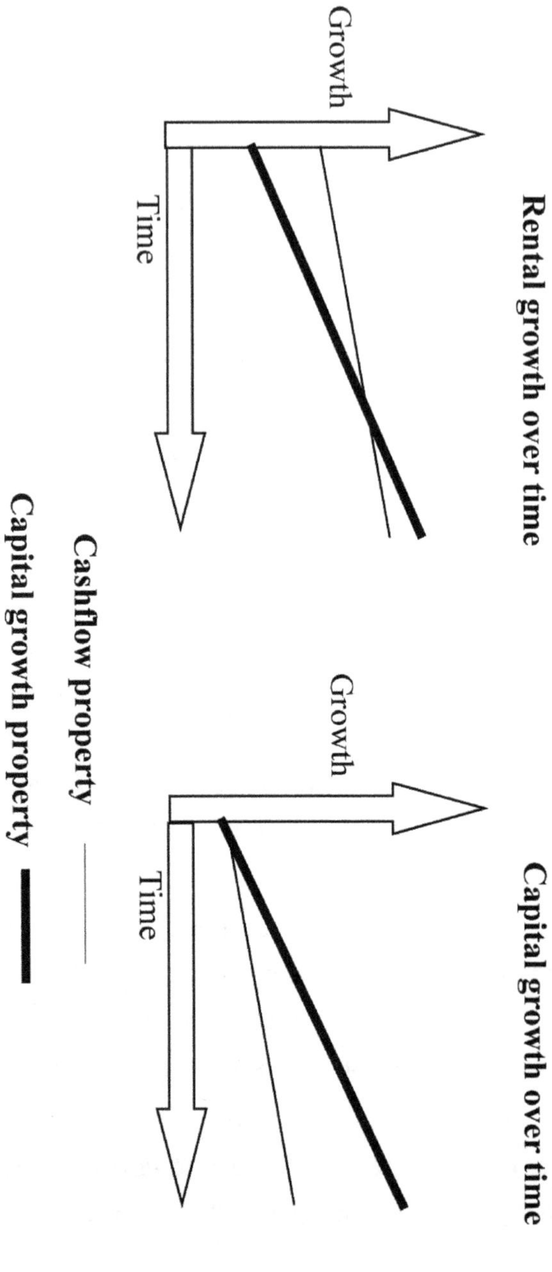
Rental growth over time
Growth
Time
Capital growth over time
Growth
Time
Cashflow property
Capital growth property

Well-located investment-grade properties will be in short supply, and rents will have more upwards pressure over the long-term, eventually surpassing the investment that was purchased simply due to a high rental yield.

There are of course going to be exceptions with exceptionally unique apartments or townhouses, where supply of a similar product is greatly limited.

8

MORE MONEY, MORE PEOPLE, A FIXED SUPPLY OF LAND

Australia is a vast, resource-rich country that is the envy of much of the world's population. Our unique resource position and stable political system draws international investment from all over the world, and we can see this in the property prices of Sydney and Melbourne, where locals are now competing for property at international price levels.

Australia's population is approximately 26.3 million people in 2023, and it is forecast to increase to over 34 million over the next twenty years, according to the Australian Bureau of Statistics. Considering it took centuries to reach 26.3 million, a further 8 million in twenty years is an exponential rate of growth.

And this isn't solely from the rate of natural increase.

This includes skilled migrants, whose benefit to the receiving economy cannot be underestimated.

As these skilled migrants find employment, they require housing (statistically they begin by renting), they pay tax, they spend money, and the economy grows.

Whether by natural increase or immigration, where are all these people going to live? How do we forecast where they will live so we know that our investment property will be in high-demand long into the future?

One answer to this question may be found in a single word. And it's the first thing that migrants look for when deciding where to live, and the first thing most people will require when they turn eighteen.

Employment

Where will the future jobs be? What industries are expanding, and will be able to afford increasing wages as technological advancements transform the workplace?

These expanding industries will almost certainly be situated in our capital cities and larger regional hubs, as this is where most of the population and wealth is already located. Smaller towns, isolated, tourism-dependent or single-industry towns are likely to suffer over the long-term, as wages and growth under-perform and the supply of land is abundant.

Well-located properties within commutable access to a range of growing industries will attract the most demand, from both renters and buyers long into the future.

Owner-occupiers will continue to pay a premium to live within a reasonable commute to work, just as renters will continue to compete to secure the right rental property within a reasonable commute to their work.

These two scenarios both lead to higher demand, while the supply of land is fixed.

Higher prices are the result.

9

TURBOCHARGING YOUR PORTFOLIO

The first step that must be understood in order to accelerate your property investing is to look at the expenses involved. With an understanding of the expected expenses a property will incur, and the costs of holding a large portfolio, you can build your portfolio in the most efficient way possible and maximise the long-term cash flow.

There are six major ongoing expenses for stand-alone houses: **Rates, Insurance, Land tax, Management, Maintenance** and the **Mortgage**.

Rates

Rates for your property are comprised of council rates and water rates.

Council rates are charges issued by the local government based on the category and value of your property. Each council has their own policy that determines how rates will be calculated. Rates are charged to pay for:

- Sports and recreation services
- Public health services
- Libraries
- Waste services
- Walking tracks
- Footpaths
- Bins
- Emergency services
- Community services and more.

Council rates vary greatly depending on the value of the land and specific local council. When estimating rates charges, you must first find out how your local council calculates rates. Most commonly, it will be based off the value of your land. You should be able to get an understanding of how much your rates commitment will be annually on your local council's website.

As rule of thumb, for an established residential property worth $400,000 - $800,000, council rates are usually $2,000 - $3,500 per annum.

Water rates are charges by the State or Territory's local water authority.

Water rates are comprised of **usage charges** and **service charges**. Usage charges are usually passed onto the tenant, and this can be confirmed on the lease agreement between the tenant and landlord. Service charges are the landlord's responsibility and these are generally very low expenses – up to a few hundred dollars per year.

Council and water rates are ongoing, fixed expenses that don't have the wiggle room of many other expenses. Local Government Areas (LGA's) that have slightly higher rates should not be a reason to not buy into a particular market, should the other characteristics of the location show strong growth trends and be well-primed for growth.

Insurance

Insurance will cover you for replacing a damaged window, to lost rent if the tenant defaults, to replacing an entire building after a natural disaster. It's your choice on the extent of your insurance, which will vary depending on your policy and insurer.

There's actually quite a bit of flexibility with insurance costs that you can play around with, negotiate, and adjust as required.

The most common types of insurance for property investors are **building insurance** and **landlord insurance**.

If you have a mortgage on your property, then your lender will require you to have building insurance for the property. It is common for the lender to want to see a Certificate of Currency given by your insurer prior to approving the loan and completing settlement. Ensure the 'sum insured' or 'building replacement value' is high enough with plenty of buffer room, so that the lender is satisfied and you have added safety if things go wrong. Lenders also like to see a high level of what is known as 'public liability insurance', which is commonly included in either of these two insurance types.

The yearly cost of building insurance can be tweaked to suit your own budget and circumstances, and in many cases, you can opt to pay monthly, rather than all in one hit. Other ways include:

- Increasing or reducing the excess (the fixed amount you have to pay if an incident or damage occurs and you want the insurer to cover the cost);
- Increasing or reducing the 'sum insured' or 'building replacement value';

- Having multiple policies with the one insurer;
- Speaking with an insurance broker to find you the best deal.

Other factors that affect the yearly building insurance premium include:

- The location (think flood zones, isolated areas, cyclone occurrences);
- The size of the build;
- The age of the property;
- The security systems in place;
- The material of the build;
- Large periods of inoccupancy.

So, what is landlord insurance?

Landlord insurance is for more specific things in relation to the property being an investment. Typical insurable events include:

- Loss of rent if the tenant defaults;
- Stolen goods;
- Malicious damage to property;
- Legal expenses if you have to evict a tenant;
- Replacement locks if you have to evict a tenant.

Landlord insurance is not always a requirement by the lender for your investment property, as they are more invested in the condition of the property covered by building insurance. However, sometimes these two types of insurances are bundled together and you get both under the one policy.

The necessity for taking out landlord insurance can be reduced by buying the correct property, choosing a great property manager, and selecting the right tenant to reside in your property.

Land tax

This is a highly controversial, highly volatile subject with the potential to increase significantly in any given year: land tax.

Currently, each state and territory have their own method of calculating how much land tax an investor will pay on the regular. If you own a property worth $700,000, the land component may be worth $400,000 and the building itself may be worth $300,000, and so the land tax payable will be based on the sum of $400,000.

Laws will change how and when this tax is payable, but the current environment means we can reduce our land tax commitment with a savvy buying strategy from the get-go.

This calculation is currently based on the total land value of all properties held in the same entity, in any given state or territory. As you can see by the table on the following page, land tax tends to increase exponentially in certain states, which can have a significant impact on our cash flow position as our properties grow in value.

There are many variables that can alter this final taxable amount for any given property, but as a general overview of the current tax rates and thresholds, we can see why diversification and being an interstate investor can greatly reduce our ongoing land tax commitment.

Approximate land tax by State and Territory, as of April 2023

State/Territory	General tax-free threshold	$500,000 of land	$1,000,000 of land	$2,000,000 of land
NSW	Up to $969,000	$0	$596	$16,596
QLD	Up to $599,999	$0	$4,500	$21,000
VIC	Up to $299,999	$775	$2,975	$12,475
SA	Up to $534,000	$0	$3,040	$20,550
ACT	No tax-free threshold	$3,399.08	$6,265.08	$12,040.08
TAS	$99,999.99	$1850	$9,350	$24,350
WA	$300,000	$780	$2,730	$14,930
NT	No land tax	$0	$0	$0

Property Management

Your investment properties should be professionally managed. Once you have found a great property manager, hand over the keys to them, pay the small fees they charge, and relax knowing your property is in safe hands. Don't believe that property management is simply just collecting rent and preparing lease agreements.

Property management is a time-consuming job and can be very stressful. Some other tasks that property managers will carry out include:

- In-going and out-going inspections;
- Routine inspections;
- Organise tradesmen (quotes and repairs);
- Tenant selection and vetting;
- Open homes;
- Regular weekly/fortnightly/monthly statements to the owner;
- Yearly End of Financial Year (EOFY) statements to the owner for ease at tax time;
- Effective online advertising;
- Handling tenant inquiries;
- Ensuring the property remains legally compliant;

- Rent reviews.

Not only is there the time and work factor, but a property management company will allow for a wider range of potential tenants to know about your property, which will create a higher demand and more applications to choose from. This will ensure the best tenant resides in your property, keeping it clean, tidy, and paying the rent on time.

Maintenance

Unfortunately, maintenance is a part of the property investing game and needs to be budgeted for, depending on the specific property purchased. For newer properties, it's important to know the builder or company and their track-record in business. The quality of the fixtures and fittings used, and any appliances installed should be of reasonable quality. Be careful not to make the mistake of thinking that all new properties will have no maintenance or defects.

As a property ages, the maintenance requirements will increase – however, there are things to look for to minimise the potential maintenance issues before buying the property. Just like your car, properties that have been treated well and kept to a reasonable standard over the years will have far less ongoing maintenance concerns than a similarly aged, neglected property.

Initially, we need to consider the build type and age. Many investors predominantly target brick builds for their sturdiness and longevity, and they can have slightly lower insurance premiums than other construction materials.

Regardless of when the property was built, we like to know if the property has been cared for over the years, if maintenance issues have been promptly carried out, and if preventative maintenance measures have been implemented.

Long-term owner-occupied or long-term sole tenant properties will generally have been taken care of better than a rental property that has had high tenant turnover.

Having a property manager inspect the property prior to purchase can be a great way to pick up on any future maintenance costs. Property managers deal with maintenance issues day-in day-out, so why not use this expertise to your advantage?

By buying an established home in a great location, we are likely to achieve higher capital and rental growth over time as opposed to a poorly located newer home, as it is the power of the land that drives price over the long-term.

However, not all maintenance problems are a bad thing.

Before a property is sold, the buyer should be aware of the maintenance issues of the property, as this cost can usually be negotiated off the purchase price - even after an offer is accepted. This is a negotiating gambit called nibbling, where small concessions are likely to be approved to get the deal over the finish line.

Properties with some work required commonly see slightly less demand than a fully renovated, set-and-forget type property – which can be a great opportunity to the investor. By using this to our advantage, we can spend less upfront, pay for repairs and basic cosmetic renovations, and create a higher value and rental return soon after purchase.

These renovations are usually cosmetic work, for example, painting (property investment gold), new carpets, window fittings/fixtures, new lighting, cleaning, and adding a carport or basic landscaping. Say you budget $15,000 for the maintenance and renovations. Upon completion, the property is likely to attract more interest from tenants, with a higher rental return, less future work to carry out, and, hopefully, an equity boost for the property of between $20,000 to $30,000 plus. This can also be a good time to organize professional photography for your property in order to maximise future online marketing campaigns.

Another benefit of cosmetic renovating is that when you want to use the initial property to buy another, the bank may send out a valuer to put a dollar figure on your property, and you want the property looking as good as possible. You want the valuer to compare your property with other high-quality homes, and not to classify it as your typical 'investment stock'.

Mortgage

Not many people buy real estate with cash, and from an investment returns point of view it doesn't always make sense. Most people save their deposit, or use just enough equity in their existing properties to put fifteen to twenty per cent down, plus purchasing costs to pay little or no Lenders Mortgage Insurance (LMI).

LMI is an expense that the buyer pays if they borrow more than eighty per cent of the purchase price, which is designed entirely to protect the bank, not the borrower. LMI will vary between borrowers, the term of the loan, and the size of the deposit. As seen in the chart below, the rate of LMI jumps sizably once the borrowed amount reaches around the 88 Loan-to-Value Ratio mark.

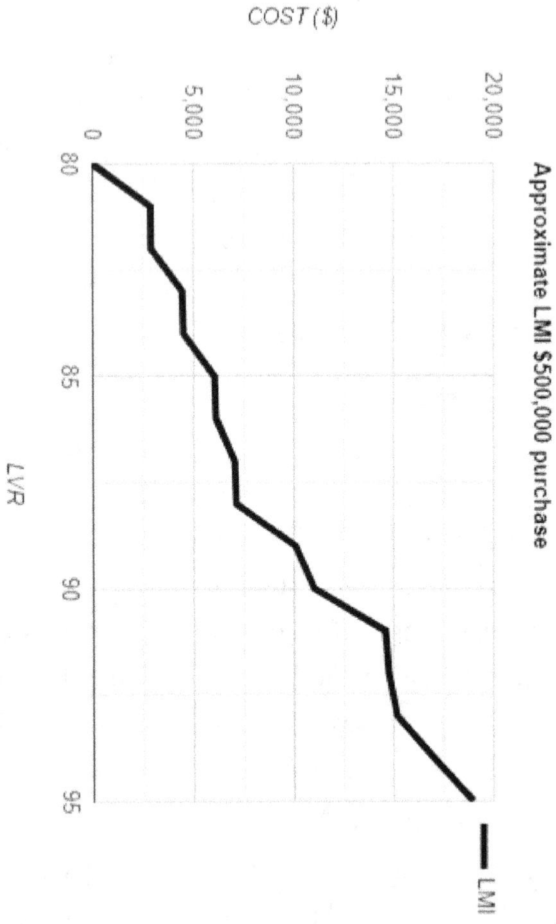

LMI is an expense that can be added to the mortgage or paid entirely upfront. The mortgage is likely to be the highest holding cost for the property, for a long time. The good news is that this expense is quite flexible. There are a number of things that can be done to help reduce your mortgage repayments:

- The loan can be refinanced to get a more competitive interest rate;
- The loan can be refinanced to extend the life of the loan to lower the regular repayments;
- The borrower can contact the lender and ask for a rate reduction;
- The interest rate can be fixed, variable, or a combination of both to suit your needs;
- The loan can be paid on an Interest-Only (IO) basis or Principal and Interest (PI) to help with cash flow requirements;
- An offset account can be set up to reduce the interest payments;
- An interest-free credit card can be set up to maximise the use of the offset account;

More on this in Chapter 15, 'Rapid mortgage reduction strategies'

Having a mortgage can seem daunting, especially to new investors. Entering into a mortgage should actually be an exciting time. You've made a plan and taken the plunge. Now let your properties do all the heavy lifting for you.

10

MAKE FINANCIAL FREEDOM POSSIBLE

Regardless of how we decide to build our property portfolio, what's the end goal that we are looking to achieve?

- More passive income for a better quality of life;
- More time to spend with friends and family;
- To have more choices and more freedom;
- To holiday more often;
- More capacity to help people;
- To create generational wealth to pass on to our children;
- To buy fancy things;
- To reduce or eliminate money problems for good.

But what income from the property exactly affords us the ability to achieve any of those things? You might be thinking 'well it must be the rental income from all the properties' – and this is partly true. But there is a lesser-known advantage to capital growth that not all investors are aware of.

Living off equity

Imagine you've accumulated your portfolio and now own four investment-grade properties. Given enough time in the market, let's say the portfolio is worth $5 million and returning $150,000 in income after all expenses. With an average portfolio growth rate of seven point five per cent, this means that the following twelve months your portfolio may be worth $5,375,000. Now you have a choice: do you leave the portfolio to continue on and simply enjoy your passive income from collected rent? Or, do you go back to the bank and tell them that you want an equity release of $150,000 because your properties have increased $375,000 in value?

Would you be concerned about taking on a manageable amount of debt when your properties and rents are growing much, much faster than the equity you are releasing?

You will then have access to this tax-free $150,000. This financial freedom strategy is called 'living off equity', and although there are many more factors to consider along the way, this is an overview of how it can be achieved.

Ensure that your overall portfolio has enough of a safety buffer to weather recessions and periods of vacancy, and thoughtfully release the right amount of equity to keep your debt controlled.

Property selection is absolutely critical to get right from the start. A poor property purchase can set back your investing timeline by years, even a decade.

11

HELP ME NARROW DOWN SOME OPTIONS OF WHAT TO BUY!

Sometimes we focus on more in-depth topics in property, when a lot of people just want some clear guidance on what kind of property would make a great investment for them.

The first step in determining what type of property will outperform the rest over the long-term is to look at some simple data provided by the big research companies. Companies like CoreLogic, SQM research, and ABS data, for example, are exceptional for providing this kind of information.

According to CoreLogic, house values across the combined capital cities are up 453% over the past 30 years to 2022, whereas unit values are up 307%.

This disconnect is also prevalent across regional Australia.

Price rises and falls are dictated by supply and demand, and with houses on good blocks taking up far more land than most units, the supply is more limited, and the long-term trends are clear.

Units can make for great lifestyle choices, but when it comes to investing, most of them significantly under perform. Supply can suddenly increase as nearby land gets developed and turned into a new residential tower or unit-block. Suddenly, your unit is one of hundreds, but not as desirable than the brand-new flashy units over the road. You might need to drop the rent or the sale price to incentivise a tenant or buyer.

Some units can make for great investments, but they will need to be exceptionally unique, without the possibility of a swathe of similar stock entering the market. Think larger 3 or 4 bedroom apartments, unique water views, or across from nature reserves to keep the future development low.

For most beginning investors, let's steer clear of units.

With the broad outperformance of stand-alone houses, here at JSC Property Investments we specialise in targeting stand-alone houses, with very rare cases of high yielding townhouses or units, depending on the clients' circumstances.

Budget will be the most limiting with our options, but even low budgets have great opportunities, if you know where to look. If you are unsure about what your budget might be, speak with a qualified mortgage broker or your bank.

Why else would we choose a stand-alone house over a unit?

- A house on a good block will tend to have more future development potential, making your block more desirable to a wider range of potential buyers in the future.

- No body corporate or strata fees. Not only can these fees increase every year, but disagreements can occur within the complex, wasting time and causing stress to rectify ongoing issues. Ensuring we keep unnecessary expenses down will have a significant impact once we have an established property portfolio.

- Opportunity for value-add work. Houses tend to have far greater value-add potential, whether it's from internal renovations (cosmetic or structural), external renovations / additions, or landscaping. Many of these options are severely limited with townhouses, units, and other properties with communal spaces/amenities.

- Zoning changes. A change of zoning (for example, from low-density residential to medium or high-density residential), will potentially cause a significant uplift in a property's value. If the zoning change allows for increased development, alterations, additions or change-of-use entirely, the block is likely to become far more valuable from a development standpoint. Developers and investors can afford to pay more for the property knowing their expected returns if the block were to be fully developed to its 'highest and best use'.

New vs established property

To be completely clear, buying an established property doesn't mean buying a 1930s dilapidated cottage with duct tape holding the ceiling together and a bucket under the rusted gutters that must be regularly emptied.

We usually stick to 1990s builds or newer, with some exceptions for the right property. This is why I've chosen the more suitable 'new versus established', rather than the common debate of 'new versus old'.

Going over some reasons why investors choose to go down the brand-new property path, let's start with the first one: high rental return.

Most new properties, once complete, will draw a premium rental return. Initially, this can be incredibly appealing and useful for our cash flow, but we need to know if it will be equally impressive in a decade's time. Once the property is no longer brand new, other properties will be the latest and greatest, and they will be receiving the premium rents.

The high rent upfront is kind of like a quick hit of adrenaline.

The fundamentals of supply and demand will be the drivers of rental growth, and the initial high rental return may stagnate for many years if the property is not in the right location.

There is an even bigger reason why so many people sign the dotted line of an off-the-plan apartment or a house and land package. It's so obvious it slaps you in the face the second one of those thousands of paid ads enters your field of view.

And that reason is incentives.

Imagine if you owned a problem property, you couldn't find a tenant, you couldn't find a buyer, but you HAD to find someone, and quickly, to pay you some rent or buy your lemon. Your advertising hasn't worked yet, you're clearly asking too much money for the current market.

It's time to offer some incentives.

For a rental advertisement:

FREE RENT FIRST MONTH

HALF RENT FIRST 6 MONTHS

ANY LEASE PERIOD CONSIDERED

MAKE AN OFFER

For a sales advertisement:

ANY OFFERS CONSIDERED

FLEXIBLE SETTLEMENT CONDITIONS

VENDOR WILLING TO FINANCE DEPOSIT

PLEASE, PLEASE BUY THIS MONEY PIT

I would advise against using the last one.

So, what incentives should be offered to buying a brand-new property?

NO OR LOW STAMP DUTY

LOW DEPOSIT

RENTAL GUARANTEE

TAX SAVINGS

Sounds like you're on to a pretty good thing! I like the thought of stamp duty savings, saving less for a deposit, having guaranteed rent, and paying a little less tax.

It certainly grabs your attention. Almost like it is intentionally directing your attention away from something else.

And it's well-known that dangling the lure of a free lunch is a typical con artist's trick. You aren't too naïve to think that these offers are made on good faith alone.

What are you hiding behind those shiny, tempting incentives, Mr Government, Mr Developer, Mr Property Marketer, and Mr Salesperson?

The price.

Every professional that is involved in the process up until the brand-new property is sold is getting paid somehow. And that somehow is added on to the actual cost of the property, funded entirely by the overly-generous buyer. We aren't talking about simply a few thousand dollars on top of the actual cost, by the way. A lot of professionals want to make big commissions on every property to make the venture worthwhile for them.

A lot of investors also see the purchase price as high, but maybe not as high as they would expect given all of these extra commissions they will be paying. The answer is simple: quietly reduce the amount of the land offered per property. This brings the cost down significantly, to make it seem like fair market value.

That's why blocks these days seem to get smaller and smaller. It hides the artificially inflated sale price and makes a lot of people who aren't you a hell of a lot of money.

And if there's one thing that makes a property investment-grade, it's a good land component.

And that's what's missing from most of these new builds.

But I still get those incentives, right?

Yes. Let's talk about them.

NO OR LOW STAMP DUTY

This is a government incentive. As new properties are purchased by investors, this brings more stock to the market, encourages more building, more jobs, and of course more tax dollars. It also assists with the rental problems which helps parties get re-elected. There is nothing sinister here, but there lies some motivation behind such a generous offer.

LOW DEPOSIT

This incentive is designed to market the product to a wider market – those with less savings. Yes, you will save on some upfront costs by buying brand-new with a low deposit incentive. There is also the potential that you will be asked to fork out tens of thousands more before the build is complete, with months or even years of delays.

Overpaying for a property to save on a deposit is like overpaying for a product to get free shipping. The extra price is simply built-in anyway.

RENTAL GUARANTEE

Australia has a perpetual shortage of rental accommodation, and many fully developed suburbs just don't have the available land to increase the market's rental stock. With a rising population, limited supply, and extremely low vacancy rates, a well-located property asking fair market rent will have a number of tenancy applications to choose from. Find peace of mind in the location of your property.

Also, with respect to rental guarantees, some companies will then manage these properties over the course of the rental guarantee. Check the management agreement and make sure that they charge fair management costs for that particular area.

TAX SAVINGS

Another government incentive of course - it's time for another hit of adrenaline. Your biggest tax savings will be in the first year, coincidentally lining up perfectly with a get-rich-quick type mindset. A brand-new property will have solid depreciation (tax-saving) benefits, which are incredibly effective at keeping attention off a heavily inflated sale price, or better investments in investment-grade locations, where capital growth is completely untaxed unless sold.

Taking more of a deep-dive into the differences of new vs established, consider:

- Location;
- Land size;
- Supply;
- Cost;
- Value-adding;
- Long-term results.

Comparison #1: Location

Location, location… what was the last one?

The most important of all is the location of the property. Buying into a new estate will generally mean that you are buying far from the CBDs, the employment hubs, the established infrastructure, the shorter commutes, the best schools, and everything else that a great, established suburb has to offer.

Comparison #2: Land size

Most new builds today are cookie-cutter type builds designed to fit as many houses as possible on the smallest possible block. The result is a poor land-to-asset ratio – meaning that most of your investment dollars are going into the materials and the cost of the build, not the land. This reduction in land size will also reduce the long-term demand for the property, affecting future capital and rental growth.

Finding a great land component to maintain long-term demand in an established property is easily achievable. You have the ability to select the appropriate land size for a suburb, or buy larger blocks with potential for future development or sub-division.

Comparison #3 Supply

With the release of a new estate and potentially hundreds of near-identical houses, it's easy to see that there will be oversupply problems, particularly in the short- to medium-term. This supply is in the form of rental availability and sales availability, so both growth aspects will be impacted.

Supply considerations need to be considered for all potential investment properties, and new estates are no exception.

Buying established properties provide further options in making the most of your ability to buy in areas with low supply and increasing demand. Desirable suburbs with high owner-occupier presence means less rental and sales availability, as owner-occupiers don't tend to sell up as often as investors.

Without the limitations of searching only for new builds, you can tailor your purchase to a location with low vacancy rates, limited amount of land for future supply, and the right mix of owner-occupiers to renters.

Comparison #4 Cost

New builds typically have a fixed price tag. This ensures that any developers, builders, agents, or third parties make enough money for the project to be viable – as detailed earlier. Upon completion of the build, there is a painfully real possibility that the property's value will be less than what the buyer paid for the property. Without modest growth to make up for this loss, this situation can be detrimental to an investor's portfolio.

Not only will this situation require time to make up for the loss, but your lender will see the property as a higher risk if you were unable to meet the repayments. They want to be comfortable that they could quickly sell the property to clear the debt if required.

The fixed purchase cost also takes away the unique ability for an investor to negotiate, to take advantage of any negative market sentiment, or to buy off-market opportunities or distressed sales which can significantly accelerate an investors' portfolio.

Comparison #5 Value-adding

Value-adding, such as renovating, landscaping, developing, sub-dividing, or improving are extremely limited with new builds. This means that if you want the growth in your property to fully fund the next purchase, then the only option available is to wait.

The value-adding options for established properties are almost endless. You can keep it simple with some basic cosmetic renovations to increase value and rental return, or you can do more in-depth work by creating an open-plan living, adding bedrooms, bathrooms, etc. With correct asset selection, basic market timing, and value-adding, you can significantly reduce the time required to leverage one property into the next.

What's so great about the available options is that the value-adding can be suited to the individual; to suit their circumstances, goals, and risk profile. At the same time, a freshly renovated property will attract more market interest, usually providing more tenancy applications, therefore more choices for a high-quality tenant who will treat the property with a higher level of care.

Comparison #6 Long-term results

A new property will provide great tax-saving benefits, high rental return, and hopefully low maintenance fees. Over time, all of these benefits effectively reduce. If you've chosen the wrong location, or bought in an area with an abundant supply of similar homes, the investment may struggle to show any real outperformance in growth moving forward.

Long-term compounding capital and rental growth will eventually outweigh these short-term benefits.

Unlike many other assets, historical performance is a useful indicator of future performance when it comes to property. By researching the past forty-year, twenty-year, ten-year, five- and three-year performance of a location, we can use the trends to estimate the potential value in the future.

Then, looking at the current fundamentals of the location (see Chapter 13), select a property that will outperform the rest of the market.

Simple!

It's not so easy to look back at twenty years of price performance of vacant land that is yet to be subdivided into small blocks and sold to the public.

It almost feels like speculation.

The result of correct asset selection after ten to twenty years can mean a difference of hundreds of thousands of dollars, a significantly larger portfolio, far more passive income, and financial freedom years sooner.

To sum up, the following factors all need to be considered when deciding whether to buy new or established properties:

New

- High supply and smaller blocks can lead to less overall growth;
- Usually marketed by developers and spruikers as a great investment – usually accompanied by incentives;
- Fixed price with all commissions factored in;

- Typically, more time required for capital growth to leverage into more assets;
- Minimal value-add options;
- Usually located in less desirable locations with lower land values, where they will be more easily sold;
- Higher price volatility. Most of these properties will have new mortgages secured against them, so these markets will be more susceptible to economic turbulence and interest rate increases.

Established

- Ability to buy into high-growth locations with good land components, ensuring strong growth in-line with the suburb;
- Ability to pay fair market value or less, saving exorbitantly high commission fees from new developer stock, and preventing any value-decline right after purchase;
- Ability to choose a location with short-term growth potential, combining with value-add methods to quickly leverage into more assets;

- More market stability with higher percentages of fully-owned properties or properties with low mortgages, immune to interest rate increases or economic uncertainty;
- More flexibility in location.

You need to ensure there is a good land content for every purchase to suit a range of future buyers and tenants, underpinning the long-term performance of the property.

To get long-term outperformance of capital and rental growth, well-located houses on great blocks have proven time and again that they outperform the rest of the market.

At the end of the day, you want a property with scarcity, uniqueness, and in a fully developed suburb with limited future supply. This can be in the form of an established, or new property. If you do decide to buy brand new, then buying a block of land and going direct to a reputable builder might just save you a small fortune.

Regional vs capital city

Regional versus capital city comparisons might seem black and white, but a long-term growth rate of a given city is only an aggregate measure and doesn't mean that every suburb will perform accordingly.

Some capital city suburbs will outperform the average, and some will underperform.

Some regional market suburbs will outperform the average, and some will underperform.

Regardless of choosing regional or capital, the suburb and asset selection are critical to a high performing investment.

Assume Brisbane, QLD has grown at eight per cent per annum over the past forty years. This means that some suburbs may have grown at nine per cent per annum, and others may have only grown at six to seven per cent per annum.

And there is a huge resulting price difference in these percentages.

When deciding on regional or capital, determine the overarching long-term growth rates of the city, and how the suburbs within your budget have fared in conjunction with this long-term trend. Have they outperformed or underperformed?

If they have underperformed, then there may be an underlying supply and demand issue. Perhaps the suburb is far away from essential services and lifestyle drivers, or perhaps there has been added supply to the market over time soaking up the existing demand.

If they have outperformed, this might mean that there is limited land available for new supply to be added to the market, or demand is continually higher due to the lifestyle benefits of the location.

There's a town called Morawa, in Western Australia, that not many people will have ever heard of. It is a mining town, with some reliance on farming and agriculture to keep the local economy afloat. The population is under a thousand people.

It's a no-brainer to steer clear from property investing in such a location.

It's a regional location that has and will continue to underperform over the long-term, because it doesn't have the qualities that make up an investment-grade location. In 1993, the median house price was only $20,000. Fast-forward 30 years and the median house price is now $77,000, according to www.pricefinder.com.au.

That's a long-term annual increase of about four point six per cent. Not a great result.

Now take Geelong, considered 'regional' Victoria. Geelong's median house price in 1993 was

$100,000. Fast-forward 30 years and the median house price is now $855,000, according to www.pricefinder.com.au.

That's a long-term annual increase of about seven point four per cent, not bad for a regional city. Some suburbs in Geelong performed even better over that time period.

According to the Australian Bureau of Statistics, the average house price in Perth in 1993 was a mere $115,000. Here in 2023, the number has increased to about $700,000.

That's a long-term annual increase six point two per cent. It looks like Geelong won this round.

Certain regional cities with all the fundamentals can perform exceptionally well, and still might be perfectly suitable for lower budgets.

A high-performing suburb in Sydney might grow at 7.5% - 8.5% per annum over the long-term, but a median price of these suburbs won't be suitable for many people.

12

PROPERTY MARKET CYCLES

Property markets are cyclical in nature. They gradually rise and fall, and we can use this information to our advantage in our property investing.

A market may boom over five years, and the average house price may have nearly doubled. It's quite likely that the market is approaching a top with such recent, explosive growth. The location could continue to boom for a while, but other markets could be better positioned in their cycles and be much better value for money.

A general rule of thumb is that a property market will rise approximately one third of the time and stagnate or fall the other two thirds of the time.

We don't know exactly when the top will be (however, I've found exceptional benefit from the team at www.propertysharemarketeconomics.com if you want to go down that rabbit hole - truly fascinating stuff), but comparing the recent growth to the average long-term growth trends can help estimate if a market may be overcooked or not.

Looking at timing the market relative to the big picture of, say, a twenty, thirty, or forty-plus year investment time frame may seem fairly insignificant, but if we buy into a rising market or a significantly undervalued market, it can give us a short-term equity boost to assist with purchasing more properties and completing a portfolio many years sooner.

Every property market has its own cycle. One suburb to the next can be at slightly different stages, and this can be observed in both the long-term and short-term price history, along with some other data trends, such as:

- Auction clearance rates;
- Days on market;
- Percent stock on market;
- Average vendor discount;
- Online search interest;
- Gross rental yields;
- Vacancy rates.

Vacancy rates can be analysed to show where the market may be in its cycle. A low, or trending lower vacancy rate means that there is upwards pressure on rents, and higher returns tend to lead to higher prices.

Historically, an asset with increasing income potential doesn't tend to lead to detrimental price crashes. This might be hard to believe given the housing situation in Australia in in 2023, where many suburbs have been declining, yet rents are increasing rapidly.

Historically, this is a more medium to long term trend, rather than one in the immediate future.

Economists and analysts like to provide a snapshot of an entire cities' growth period, but as previously elaborated upon, this is not an accurate metric as to the performance of every suburb in a given city. Some investment-grade suburbs may be at the beginning of their rising market phase, while others may have already reached their peak. This is why such a broad metric can be misleading if an investor were to buy into the wrong suburb, in a city they believed to be starting its growth phase.

As markets move through their cycles, people tend to extrapolate the past two years as the definite future. By understanding the overarching cycles at play, you can use this market sentiment to your advantage. For an extremely in-depth history of property cycles and understanding where we are now, I would highly recommend *The Secret Life of Real Estate and Banking* by Phil Anderson, *The Secret Wealth Advantage* by Akhil Patel, *Boom Bust* and *The Power in the Land* by Fred Harrison. If you don't mind a deep dive into property cycles and understanding where we are now in the cycle, I'd start with *The Secret Life of Real Estate and Banking*.

How the media helps with your investing

As markets rise, fall, or simply stagnate, you will notice the hyperbole in the news about what is going on in the property market.

The media is usually quite a bit later than reality, by several weeks or even months. Any price declines or increases are greatly emphasised, with psychological tricks to capture as much attention as possible.

Catchy media headlines actually exacerbate the property cycles, making the booms and busts stronger and more damaging than they would otherwise be. The most popular news stations in the country have a tremendous power to influence and persuade the masses as they see fit, with the only goal in mind to increase viewership and clicks.

‘Loss Aversion’ in behavioral economics essentially means that a person’s fear of loss is stronger than their desire to gain, if the resulting amounts are equal in nature. For this reason, news stations will see increased numbers in viewers with the fear-promoting headlines rather than the good-news headlines.

Fear and irrationality sell. Optimism and rationality do not.

It's just reality.

The biggest news stations should be looked at in a different light when it comes to property investing advice. And that's a very dark light, where you can't actually see the nonsense that they are telling you.

This is not to say that the news is entirely wrong when it comes to property investing, but know that if you invest according to what the media is telling you, your results will also be the same as the vast majority of investors.

And about ninety per cent of investors never make it past one or two investment properties.

Buying counter-cyclically

Over the long term, well-located investment-grade properties have performed exceptionally well, many of them rising from seven to nine per cent per annum when averaged out over a long period of time. Knowing this, and knowing the locations where we can expect these results, why not buy an investment-grade property counter-cyclically?

A stagnant or falling market can mean only one thing – demand is too low. This can give you the advantage of being the only competitive buyer for a property, as sellers fight for a buyer who holds all the cards.

Many people bought property in the early stages of the COVID-19 crisis, and I suspect many were well versed on market cycles, and many of them would have picked up properties at a sizable discount. As our country exited the recession, sentiment improved and, as history shows, the market exploded out of its stagnant period and into solid growth once again.

This is the power of buying counter-cyclically, and when sentiment is largely negative.

If you are in a safe position to buy an investment property, but there is some degree of fear in the market holding you back (rising interest rates, high inflation, price corrections), then you can be sure that many others are thinking the same thing.

Will you take advantage of this lower competition?

If a location has had very low to stagnant growth over the past ten or so years, it may be close to becoming a rising market. Take Australia's third biggest city, Brisbane, for example. While Sydney and Melbourne boomed from 2011 to 2018, Brisbane was left behind and showed negligible growth over the same period (some inner-city locations excluded). However, looking at the past forty to fifty years in Brisbane, the median house price has actually increased approximately eight per cent per annum over the long-term.

The city was clearly in its declining/flat stage of the cycle and was well positioned for a period of strong growth, which began in late 2020 and early 2021. This period of growth for Brisbane is likely to continue for years, and even with temporary setbacks from rising interest rates and economic uncertainty, in 2023, Brisbane still presents as an undervalued market well due for its time in the sun.

Another example of the power of buying counter-cyclically can be seen in the regional city of Orange, NSW, in the couple of years preceding 2016. The city's property growth was flat for roughly a decade, yet before this there was a significant boom in prices. The city's vacancy rates were trending lower year-on-year, infrastructure projects were being proposed, hospitals and government departments were in the early stages of development, properties were selling quicker, and auction clearance rates were picking up.

The city was experiencing a shift in sentiment, and a confidence not seen in a long time. Many property owners were fed up with a poorly performing property market – in this case, for around a decade - and many of them took advantage of the first change of sentiment and decided to sell. This was the worst time to make that decision.

Unfortunately for those sellers, the city was at the very beginning of its rising market phase, and over the next six or so years the average house price increased from about $300,000 to $650,000.

The lesson here: considering the market cycle is imperative for successful property investing.

Commercial property and market timing

If you decide to purchase commercial property, it's important to understand that offices, warehouses, retail shops, and other business-related properties do not follow the same cycle of residential real estate. One city's average house price may rise by $200,000, and during the same period, most of their commercial properties might not increase at all. Commercial property growth is far more linked to economic and business growth, but supply and demand are equally important across all the asset classes.

13

DUE DILIGENCE

I know what you're thinking. *Skip! I just want to buy a property.* I love your enthusiasm, but hear me out.

Due diligence is time-consuming, repetitive, and can at times be very tedious. However, avoid due diligence at your own risk. It's an integral part of the property investment game, and with such a physical, tangible asset that you claim full responsibility for, you must conduct due diligence on every single property you are considering for your portfolio.

It's for peace of mind in your investing and for your future livelihood.

If you like the thrill of the unknown or just want to hurry up and buy any property, then buy the property first and you only have to conduct due diligence once. **Nervously checking flood zone maps the day before settlement.**

I'm quite a pragmatic person, and I believe that pragmatism is needed when it comes to real estate investing. Leaving the sales pitch at home, below is some useful, clear guidance on how to conduct due diligence.

And that's what this topic is all about.

Let's dive in.

Proximity to services and infrastructure

Highways

- A residential property on a busy highway will usually have less interest from buyers and renters, therefore reducing the long-term performance of the investment. Major arterial roads can cause the same impact – have a look at any given location and compare the prices of a property on a quiet street, and one a street or two away on a busy highway.

Schools

- A great school can be a significant driving factor for price growth, especially if the catchment area is extremely limited. A house on one side of the street may be worth $100,000 more than an identical house on the other side, and have a higher rental return, and the only reason may be the school catchment area. A property in close proximity to a great school can be in-demand by many families who appreciate a safe and short journey to school for their kids.

Universities

- Easy access to a major university will see increased demand from both the employment factor and the student demographic. With an already-limited supply of housing near many universities, this extra demand can lead to significant price increases in the surrounding area. Properties being rented by-the-room tend to perform exceptionally well when situated near a major university, where the property is well-catered for the market.

Public transport

- Public transport options will definitely help to increase the demand for your investment over the long term. Ensure they are not too close in proximity, such as a busy train line across the road.

Flight paths

- Most areas won't have residential developments too close below flight paths. If the property is near an airport, check the flight paths, spend some time in the area, or check property values with neighbouring streets and suburbs and see if there is a clear disconnect in values.

Factories or industrial estates

- Properties too close to factories or industrial areas might be susceptible to excessive air pollution, noise pollution, or regular heavy vehicle traffic and general busyness.

Parks and recreation

- Nearby open spaces have been scientifically proven to have a positive impact on an area's livability factor and mental health of residents. A local park, sports field, or nature reserve will go a long way to maintaining a healthy suburb.

Healthcare

- Easy access to medical facilities is a clear draw card for an investment property. In an age where medical advancements are being made every day, the healthcare industry is rapidly expanding and will create high demand long into the future.

Childcare

- Having several childcare options nearby your investment property will make everyday life easier for families looking to rent your property. Many new families would put childcare options fairly highly on their list of rental property requirements.

Hazards of the natural environment

Flood zones

- Most council websites will have their local flood mapping tool available online. If you still aren't sure if your property is in a flood zone, run a couple of building insurance quotes on the property – insurers know which properties are in flood zones and will factor the higher risk into your quote.

Fire hazards

- Bush Bush fire prone areas can have higher insurance costs, for obvious reasons. However, with abundant reserves or nearby forests the area could be particularly limited with regards to the future supply of available housing. Consider the trade-off of higher insurance costs and future growth potential.

Cyclones and other disaster-prone areas will typically result in higher, regular insurance costs. These climatic conditions must be considered before committing to an investment property in these locations.

The suburb

Vacancy rates – A suburb's vacancy rate refers to the number of rental properties that are advertised for rent, in proportion to the total number of rental properties in the market. A low or trending lower vacancy rate means that there are fewer rental properties becoming available in an area, putting upwards pressure on rents, which eventually leads to an increase in house prices.

Increasing income returns eventually make their way into higher asset prices, not just in real estate.

Low vacancy rates not only ensure very limited periods of vacancy for your investment property, but also give the investor more choice for finding the best tenant to live in and care for your property.

Employment hubs and proximity to CBD – A property within a reasonable commute via car or public transport to large employment hubs means that your property will be in demand from a pool of potential tenants and buyers. With an increase in work-from-home culture and many people not needing to go into the office every day, this could translate into slightly longer commutes still being acceptable.

The 'ripple effect' can be used in conjunction with other data trends to find out whether a suburb is undervalued or not. Looking at the big picture, price growth tends to begin at the CBDs and ripple outwards over time.

Average household size – A suburb may have an average household size of 3.2 persons, which means that three- and four-bedroom properties are likely to be in the most demand. In this situation, two-bedroom properties may not be most suitable for finding the highest demand in the local market.

Government housing presence – Statistically, pockets of high government housing tend to correlate with higher crime rates. From an investor's point of view, you can stay away from these areas, or you can see the opportunity in this situation.

And what's that opportunity?

1 Lower prices, higher yields (when compared to surrounding suburbs)

2 Less competition to enter the market

3 Larger blocks are not uncommon, potentially sub-dividable

4. Adding security systems can have a greater impact on value-adding
5. Some of these suburbs are very well-located, and gentrification is likely to take place eventually, leading to significant growth over a shorter time period.

There are also plenty of great long-term tenants in these areas, and you can still have your set-and-forget type investment if that's your goal.

Owner-occupier presence – Owner-occupiers tend to hold their properties for longer than investors. They don't tend to sell up when recessions hit, in fact they are more likely to want to stay until there is more certainty in their future. This translates to less stock on market and less rental accommodation as the long-term supply plummets.

Owner-occupiers also tend to focus more on paying their loans down, reducing potential price volatility in times of economic uncertainty, which means fewer distressed sales and mortgagee-in-possessions.

On the flip side, there is rental presence. Higher levels of renters shouldn't be avoided altogether, as some locations are simply popular with renters. If vacancy rates are trending lower and lower, then there is supply issue and this will translate to higher rents. Eventually, it will be more cost-effective to buy than to rent, and the ratio will change.

Areas of high rental presence without the trending lower vacancy rates will usually experience more sales options and rental availability at any given time. With increasing options for buyers and tenants, this translates into an underperforming investment.

Nearby vacant or undeveloped land – what is the council zoning of this land, what might it be used for in future? If the land can be built on, it could become a new estate one day. This will add supply to the market and lower the demand for nearby properties. The zoning of the area can be checked on the local council's website.

The block

Before you dig request – An understanding of where current infrastructure is located on the block can be easily found at https://www.byda.com.au/. This quick search checks storm water pipes, sewer connections, town water connections, internet/NBN connectivity and underground or overhead cables.

Slope of the block – A reasonably flat block will be more functional than a steeper block. It might also make future building easier without the need of leveling steep areas and adding extra cost. However, if there are great views because of the elevated block, it might be worth the trade-off.

Shape of the block – The shape of the block is more important if you are looking to one day develop or subdivide. Many councils look at the blocks' frontage to the road, and require a minimum width for potential developments and subdivisions.

Size of the block – The ideal block size will vary depending on the suburb – usually reducing as you move closer to the CBD. In most cases, a good rule of thumb is to look for a minimum of $400m^2$ blocks for houses. Blocks under $400m^2$ tend to suffer greatly over the long-term with less interest from buyers and tenants who appreciate a little bit more space.

New estates in middle-ring or outer-ring suburbs of a city should contain an absolute minimum land size of $400m^2$. Unfortunately, smaller blocks than these are resoundingly common, and long-term growth is the trade-off.

The side of the street – Is there a high side and low side of the street? Do the properties on the high side have great views while the properties on the low side are missing out? This doesn't mean avoiding one side of the street entirely, just be cautious not to overpay for what you are getting.

The build

The condition of the build – Has the property been cared for and well-maintained by the current owner? Are there any issues that have been ignored that can lead to unexpected costs? A thorough inspection or two is a necessary step of due diligence. Always get a building and pest report even if the property looks immaculate throughout.

The age of the property - This data is available for most properties online, otherwise the agent or owner should be able to tell you. An older property doesn't mean $5,000+ in maintenance every year. An older neglected property means $5,000+ in maintenance every year.

The size of the build – The build size should be suitable for the local market.

A very small build might mean extra small bedrooms and living areas, potentially receiving less interest from future tenants and buyers.

A much larger build size might also see reduced demand with tenants not wanting so much maintenance, and potentially only suitable to a smaller pool of tenants. Larger builds might also end up costing the owner much more in regular maintenance costs.

14

STRUCTURING YOUR PORTFOLIO

What the heck does that mean? Structuring your portfolio? Just buy the properties and kick back. Easy.

Yes and no. Whose name will the property be in? If you're a couple looking to invest, does it go in both names? Should it go in the higher or lower income-earners name? Should you go to your accountant and set up a trust?

At the time of writing, the title can't be changed after purchase without enormous costs involved.

The lowest cost structure is simply buying in personal names, but maybe you like the sound of buying in a trust and have weighed up their pros and cons.

I would highly recommend an appointment with your accountant to discuss your personal situation and goals and which structure would be most suitable to you.

Personal names

Buying property in your own name is generally the simplest and lowest cost structure. Buying in two people's names is common, but buying in three or more people's personal names can lead to a train wreck.

There are many reasons why multiple names on a property title can lead to issues, and here are some of the biggest reasons:

1. If one of the owners wants to buy another property alone, then many lenders will only consider a portion of the rental income (one half if there are two names on the title, one third if there are three names), yet the entire loan amount against your application.

2. You will generally not be able to use the equity in that property unless it is for another joint purchase in the same people's names again.

3. Disagreements on everyday decisions for the property can occur. What if one person wants the rent increased? What if another wants to sell? What if one doesn't want to pay to renovate?

4 If the property was bought with family or friends, this can put pressure on their relationships.

Buying property in multiple names can have its benefits for short-term buying and selling, but can really throw off an investor's plans if the property is planned for a long-term buy and hold and if they want to significantly scale their portfolio.

Trusts

Trusts have a flexibility that buying in a personal name just can't compete with. They have certain tax advantages, higher levels of asset protection, and the ability to interchange who controls the trust at any time. But it comes at a cost.

A lot of extra costs, actually.

Extra cost 1: Mortgage lenders will usually charge a higher interest rate for trust properties.

Extra cost 2: Land tax may be significantly higher if purchased through a trust. See the relevant State or Territory's government websites.

Extra cost 3: Solicitor costs, set-up costs, bank fees and charges, separate tax return and accountancy costs will all be higher with a trust.

For someone new to property investing, this type of structure might seem overwhelming. A trust isn't necessary for every investor and it can have more or less benefits from one investor to the next.

If you're interested in learning more or pursuing a trust structure for your portfolio, arrange an appointment with an accountant who regularly deals with trusts and stays up-to-date with any legislative changes that regularly effect trusts.

15

RAPID MORTGAGE-REDUCTION STRATEGIES

Whether you want to pay down the mortgage on an owner-occupied home or an investment property, there are simple ways to speed up the process and get the loan paid sooner.

And this doesn't just include making extra repayments.

You may have a plan to buy a certain number of properties, let them grow, and eventually sell one or two to wipe out as much debt as possible. Debt reduction might not be the goal at this stage of the journey.

But one day it probably will be, and some of these strategies may still provide some benefit in the short-term.

Owner occupied loans vs investment property loans

The first thing to understand is that an owner-occupied mortgage is not tax-deductible. The repayments are made with after-tax dollars, and cannot be claimed back in normal circumstances.

Investment property mortgage repayments are tax-deductible (at least the interest portion of them is), along with their ongoing expenses as described previously.

This means that it is generally wise to pay the owner-occupied mortgage first. Even better, increase the investment property loans, if possible, to reduce the owner-occupied mortgage.

This will result in the same level of debt, with more tax benefits.

Regular repayments

Interest on the loan is calculated daily, so asking your bank or broker for weekly or fortnightly repayments can save small amounts on interest, which can add up to large amounts over time. At the same time, it wouldn't hurt to ask them if you are getting the best rate – they might just give you a discounted interest rate on the spot.

Offset accounts

Offset accounts are excellent tools for reducing mortgage repayments, for both investors and owner-occupiers alike. These accounts help reduce the amount of interest on the loan that you will pay, by subtracting the amount in the offset account from the loan outstanding.

Here's how it works.

If your mortgage interest rate is five point five per cent, then you will save 5.5% x $50,000 = $2,500 per year on interest that you would have otherwise had to pay.

In the above example, if you have $50,000 in your offset account linked to that loan, you will only be paying interest on $450,000. If your mortgage is $500,000, and you have $0 in the offset account, then you are paying five point five per cent interest on the entire $500,000.

Leaving a safety buffer in your offset account can give peace of mind in case of emergencies, and at the same time reducing your mortgage repayments.

Interest-free credit cards

For the most proactive investors who want to ensure their savings are making the greatest possible impact in mortgage reduction, consider setting up a zero-interest credit card linked to this offset account. This card must be regularly repaid before the interest-free period ends, and in full, to ensure no extra charges.

If you're an investor who just wants to keep things simple, then a single offset or bank account with all in-going and outgoing monies labeled with the property's address they relate to should make accountability, and your tax return, simpler.

Regularly refinance

Many banks will slowly increase the interest rate on your mortgages, even if the official cash rate has not been increased.

Cheeky devils.

Most people wouldn't continue buying groceries from Woolworths if they increased prices thirty per cent across the board. They'd shop around, go to IGA or Coles.

It's the same with your mortgage.

Never refinancing or reviewing your interest rate is accepting to pay whatever the lender wants to charge.

But you're better than that.

If your property has grown in value, or if you have paid some of the loan off, then you now have more of a safety net and more peace of mind for yourself and lender. As your loan-to-value ratio lowers, it's very possible that you will be approved for a lower interest rate.

If you've gone through a great mortgage broker, then they will keep you updated as to whether you are paying a competitive market rate, or if you can do better with a refinanced loan.

16

TAX MINIMISATION

Tax benefits are secondary to profitable property investing. A goal wholly and solely to save tax through property investing will lead you down the wrong path, and get your portfolio stuck in a rut.

This is because cash flow will be the main focus, and high-performing, fully established suburbs that will create life-changing wealth will be ignored.

You need the power of the land to do the heavy lifting and get you to the next level, not temporary tax savings.

A goal of tax-saving leads a lot of people to house and land packages and off-the-plan developments, with their tantalising tax benefits and scammy salespeople.

But remember how you subtly have to pay tens and tens of thousands of dollars in commissions just to secure them? Steer clear of the shiny tax benefits the spruikers will try to push to you. Cut the middleman away and go direct to a builder if you are set on a brand-new dwelling.

Established property may still have some depreciation benefits, and at the time of writing this is a rate of two point five per cent of the total construction costs per year for forty years. New fixtures, fittings, and renovations all have specific ATO guidelines for claiming, but generally speaking, most of these costs are tax-deductible.

In any case, a depreciation schedule might be worth paying for. This is a document that you give your accountant at tax time, and includes any depreciation benefits relating to your property. A phone call to a quantity surveyor will assist in deciding whether the upfront cost of the schedule will be worthwhile for the tax benefits.

These schedules tend to cost around $300 - $800, depending on the property.

What other main expenses are claimable with investment properties?

- Interest on the loan (the principal portion is not)
- Maintenance
- Insurance
- Council/water rates
- Property management
- Body corporate/strata

- Land tax.

As mentioned earlier, land tax can be reduced with diversification between States and Territories.

As a couple, if the property is expected to be negatively geared for many years, then it might be most tax-effective to buy in the higher income-earners name, just as a positive geared property may work better in the lower income-earners name.

Confirm with your accountant that this would be the right option for your specific situation.

If the investor is expecting to be in a lower tax bracket the following financial year, it might be worth bringing some bills forward to pay in June to get more benefit from the deduction. On the other hand, if your income is expected to be higher the following financial year, see if you can request some delayed payments until July for some expenses.

Also, keep accurate records for your property to make sure to don't miss anything at tax time. JSC Property Investment's website has a free-to-download Excel document that lists all the buying and holding costs to keep things simple and in one place. You can send this to your accountant when the time comes, keeping the entire documentation process as simple as possible.

17

POPULAR PROPERTY MYTHS

Self-managed property portfolios

Should you buy an investment property near where you live, so you can manage it?

Imagine the savings.

About $2,500 - $4,000 per year (tax-deductible), for a typical residential property.

What if you paid this money to a reputable, professional property manager who advertises the property across all the major platforms and to potential tenants in their database?

The higher demand could mean you achieve a higher rent, and perhaps a better tenant, which offsets this extra cost anyway.

Property investing should give you more freedom, not more work.

Nevertheless, does the thought of carrying out regular inspections, organising tradespeople, staying up-to-date with ever-changing legislative rental property requirements, being the first point-of-contact for your tenant at all times, physically paying council and water rates throughout the year, maintaining rental records and bond payments, following up with the tenant if they fall into arrears sound fun?

Well, property managers do all that and much more.

In ninety-nine per cent of cases, you shouldn't manage the property yourself. Your time worth more.

Buy one property, pay it off before buying another

Taking risk-aversion to the extreme, some investors might want to fully pay off a property before buying the next one.

How long might it take to repay the loan, with regular extra repayments, rapid mortgage reduction strategies, and the occasional lump-sum payment?

Fifteen years?

Twenty years?

That's a long time and potentially hundreds of thousands of growth to let pass by – as previously described.

An investor can remain conservative with their debt levels and yet still expand their portfolio. It's just a matter of not over-leveraging, and having a safety buffer for emergencies.

Overall, debt levels under seventy per cent are considered very safe. But this is arbitrary and completely up to the risk tolerance of the investor.

Buy cheap properties with high yields

This is similar to a cash flow strategy that we discussed in Chapter 7. A high yield alone isn't enough to help us create a high-performing portfolio, and we need an ongoing out-performance in capital and rental growth as time goes on.

And the cheap properties get left behind in the dust.

Rent-to-buy ~~seams~~ schemes

Rent-to-buy schemes are extremely high-risk contracts between a prospective purchaser and a seller that enables a purchaser to buy a property over an extended period of time, rather than the traditional upfront full payment on settlement that is most common today.

The purchaser lives in the property, pays rent (and sometimes maintenance and other ongoing costs), while also making extra regular payments which count as going towards the purchase of the property. This is usually accompanied by an upfront deposit - $5,000 is common – but conditions for these contracts can vary greatly.

It's a legal grey area, and not particularly favourable for the buyer who didn't write up the contract.

Over time, the buyer holds on to hope that these extra repayments create enough of a down-payment that they will be approved for a loan by a lender, before the rent-to-buy contract expires.

The clock is ticking! Everyone loves a high-pressure financial make-or-break commitment.

The most common reason buyers enter into these agreements is because they are not in a position to get a loan in the first place, where they don't have the income or the deposit available.

Or maybe they don't read through the contract that was destined to fail in the first place.

Why would the seller want the contract to not be fulfilled? Because they get to keep all the rent you paid, your upfront payment and all the other extra payments you made along the way, of course!

And predatory sellers know this. They also know that in most cases, the potential buyer won't be approved for finance when the time comes.

A 2016 study by the Consumer Action Law Centre couldn't identify a single successful rent-to-buy case.

Buy 8,000 properties in 5 years!

Eight thousand might be hyperbole, but it's always amusing to see ads or property books promoting buying dozens of properties in a few short years. Maybe it's twenty properties in three years, maybe it's fifty properties in five years, maybe it's two hundred and fifty-nine properties in seven years (sigh).

These goals are largely not achievable by the vast majority of investors in Australia's property market today. The few exceptions could be that very cheap properties are targeted, the investor is starting out with millions of dollars, extremely high-risk financing options are involved, or the law is being bent.

Many of these thought-provoking titles are simply clickbait, and your best-interests will not be their priority.

Buying several investment-grade properties will give a far greater financial result, without the high-risk and headaches. The more carefully selected your properties, the less will be required for significant wealth-creation.

A final note on these strategies – consider who stands to make the most money transacting all these properties. Is it a buyer's agent? A developer? An unlicensed property sourcing specialist?

If you ask them, they might just say "the investor makes all the money, of course!"

Tread carefully.

Buying in mining towns

I've known of professional buyers' agents who pushed properties in mining towns to their clients during the mining boom of the early 2000s. Even today, they are worth less than what they paid!

That's the cost of following the wrong advice, littered in the industry today.

The pitch might be to purchase a property for $100,000 - $200,000 and rent it out for over $300 per week. Maybe quite a bit more. What a goldmine! The price can only go one way!

When the mines pack up and leave, or when commodity prices plummet and there are lay-offs, the town instantly feels the repercussions as the money stops flowing. Vacancies increase, investors flee the market, and you're stuck with a poorly-located property with no demand seen for miles, in any direction.

And the price goes down.

There may be some price gains during the period of high commodity prices and increasing mining demand, but the boom times are evanescent, it may be worthwhile to quickly exit the market while the going is good.

Using the equity in these properties to grow your portfolio can be extremely dangerous, assuming the lender is willing to grant a further loan. This can potentially put your entire portfolio at risk with slight fluctuations in commodity demand.

Without the ability to use equity safely to further expand the portfolio, they aren't well-suited as a foundation for a long-term property portfolio.

It's a speculative venture, not for the conservative investor.

CBD apartments

Most CBD apartments have suffered dearly in recent history. With new developments popping up like dandelions in spring, over-supply problems have flooded many major CBD markets across the country.

And with this increasingly high supply, down go prices.

And up goes the vacancy rate.

CBD apartments have a volatility similar to mining towns. They can grow quickly with little warning, and the supply and demand can rapidly fluctuate.

History teaches us that they severely under-perform over the long term, when compared to a well-located investment grade property.

If an investor is set on buying a CBD apartment, then look for the right combination of uniqueness, location, supply constraints and lifestyle benefits. What makes this apartment different to the rest?

Promotional marketing headlines

"'Iron Triangle' to lead SA price growth"

This is a direct quote from a well-known property investment company, published in January of 2012.

The 'Iron triangle' is a term used to describe the iron-producing region of South Australia's industrial towns of Port Pirie, Port Augusta, and Whyalla. There was much speculation about BHP megaprojects and huge investment in the surrounding areas at the time.

According to SQM Research, Port Augusta's weekly asking sale price for houses went from $231,354 in January 2012, to $244,687 in December 2012. Stop all the clocks.

Today, the median house price for Port Augusta is anywhere from $200,000 - $250,000, depending on the data source. Wide-ranging sales at relatively low numbers tend to skew the data.

Several years later, this article came out regarding Whyalla's real estate market:

> *Whyalla residents are trapped in a real estate nightmare.*
>
> *The average time on the market for a house in the battling regional city has blown out to a whopping 248 days and many people are being forced to cut asking prices by 20 per cent.*
>
> *"The median price for houses in the six months ended December 31, 2015 fell by*

10 per cent to $215,000, and the number of sales achieved dropped in 2015 to 111, compared with 252 in 2014, said Domain chief economist Andrew Wilson."

This quote is from *The Sydney Morning Herald*, published on 12 April 2016.

Catchy headlines aren't enough as a basis for property investing.

And that leads us to the next triangle, 'The Golden Triangle'.

The Golden Triangle refers to the South-East Queensland regions of the Sunshine Coast, Gold Coast, Toowoomba, and everything in between.

Here is an excerpt from an article from news.com.au published on 1 June 2015:

"For us I see the golden triangle out to Toowoomba, up to the Sunshine Coast and down to the Gold Coast.

"Anywhere in Queensland will do well but I'd be hard pushed to find anywhere better to invest than the southeast of Queensland in the next 3-5 years for capital growth."

And this is a direct quote from the founder and CEO of McGrath Estate Agents.

South-East Queensland is a big area, with a wide range of property markets. The tagline suggests that anywhere within the triangle will see a significant increase in property prices.

It's a bold statement that didn't live up to the hype.

Many suburbs in 'The Golden Triangle' had no growth in the proceeding three to five years, in fact some were worth even less after inflation was factored in.

But some did incredibly well. Unfortunately, there was no caveat saying "very select suburbs in the golden triangle will perform exceptionally well, those where demand exceeds supply, the data corroborates a rising market, and long-term history suggest strong growth is on the horizon".

A catchy headline and media hype isn't enough to base significant investment decisions off. No growth over five years or more will make it difficult to expand your portfolio and achieve your goals!

18

NEGOTIATING SECRETS FROM A PROFESSIONAL BUYER'S AGENT

Negotiating starts from the second you start speaking to the selling agent, not when it comes time to place the offer. If you haven't planned your negotiating from the first call or email, then you may end up paying thousands more than you should have.

Agents negotiate all day, every day. They are professional negotiators whose commission and reputation are directly tied to the final sale price. An agent who consistently achieves high sale prices will gain more listings as their reputation builds, just as an agent who under-performs will see less listings as sellers choose the agent who can achieve the higher sale price.

The industry pressure is enormous.

Most people will only buy several properties in their entire lifetime. How are they supposed to know how to get the lowest sale price with these experienced professionals representing the seller?

Before getting into a practical example, let's go over some tactics to first understand before our initial contact with the agent.

Tactic #1: Playing dumb

One of the easiest, and possibly most self-entertaining tactics is playing dumb.

Playing dumb can be exceptionally rewarding, particularly in real estate investing. As humans, our guard is subconsciously lowered when we believe we are much more intelligent than the other person. This can lead to gathering more information about the property or seller than they otherwise would have revealed. We might learn that the agent is under pressure to quickly sell the property (jackpot), that there are no genuine or enticing offers on the table, or that the seller has other motives other than simply the highest sale price. Think divorces, moving interstate, or any other time-sensitive scenarios among the realm of possibilities.

And all information revealed can be used to our advantage.

In showing intelligence and perception, you might just never be told of these extra nuggets of information gold. Humans are involved with the transaction of real estate, so human psychology will play a part in achieving the best deal.

Tactic #2: Nibbling

Nibbling is a negotiating tactic where further negotiating takes place after the offer has already been agreed upon and accepted. With the time and effort committed to getting this far, neither party really wants the deal to fall through.

You might even think, *Why would I risk losing the property to a few thousand dollars when the deal is already locked in?*

Because in most cases of a negotiation, both parties believe they have a weaker negotiating position than they actually do.

And all it takes is one email.

A practical example of nibbling in buying property would be once the building and pest inspection has been carried out and you've gone through the report and minor maintenance problems are found.

They could be incredibly minor problems, no reason to walk away from a great deal.

Exaggerate the impact these problems will have for you, as the buyer, if you were unaware of them before placing the offer.

There is some rust on the fence? What a disaster!

Use hyperbole (within reason) when discussing the estimated costs of repairing all the potential maintenance problems found in the report, and list them all in your email to the agent. Let's say in this example, we request a $6,000 discount.

The agent will present the request to the seller, and one of three things are likely to happen.

1 The seller will reject the request in its entirety

2 The seller will negotiate down your request, perhaps asking to split the difference ($3,000)

3 The seller will accept your request in full.

As a professional buyer's agency, we find in most cases the seller will accept the full or partial discount. In very few instances will sellers completely reject a discount request.

Tactic #3: A higher authority

Never agree to major changes immediately after they are put to you. Request some time to think it over, or better yet, use the higher authority gambit.

Scenario

Selling agent: *"The vendor is happy with your conditions; the only problem is that the price is a little low. They have told me that if you come up another $10,000, they will be happy to sign the contract today."*

You: *"Oh (flinching)... thank you for the feedback. I'd have to ask (insert higher authority) to see if we can increase the offer at all. I'll get back to you as soon as I can. Would the vendor still consider the offer if we could only increase by $3,000-$4,000?"*

Their reply could give you all the confidence that the seller would accept a $3,000 increase, or possibly no increase at all.

This is a great tactic to use as a buyer's agent, as the higher authority is the client. It's also a great tactic for a married couple, as the higher authority can be your partner.

If you don't have a partner, the higher authority can be a friend, a business partner, a family member, even a fictional partner.

It doesn't matter at all, because we are simply biding time and digging for information.

Example gracious

Let's assume a property is advertised for sale at $599,000.

The first step is to get an in-depth understanding of the true value of the property. This can be done by checking comparable sales in the area in the past several months. Take your time at this step, consider the pros and cons of the comparable properties, the block sizes, the build sizes, age, and construction type. One comparable property may be close by, but it could be in a flood zone, a pocket of high government housing, or the less desirable side of the street. Keeping in touch with the market over time will also help in determining what the target property is worth in the current market.

Try and narrow it down to a small range. Let's say you've decided it's really worth $620,000 – $630,000 (the listed price is much more to do with human psychology rather than what the agent and seller think it is actually worth).

Now that you've decided on the true value, keep it a secret.

Assuming the inspections have gone well and the due diligence is complete and satisfactory, it's time to find out a little about the seller. Some agents are more than willing to share some broad information around the seller's motivations for selling, while other, more cautious agents will keep this information to themselves.

So, what information do we want to know, and how will it help?

We want to know what the seller wants, other than the highest sale price, to tailor the conditions of our offer.

Easy!

Conditions are a major factor at play when it comes to buying and selling property. Lower offers win the day regularly, because they have fewer, or more favourable conditions for the seller.

Ask the agent: "What are the seller's ideal offer conditions?"

We are trying to find out whether they would prefer a long or short settlement, are they buying another property and will want a lease-back until they are able to move, or if they are an investor who simply wants the shortest settlement with the best price.

There can any number of scenarios, and this is valuable negotiating information.

Confirm with your mortgage broker or lending institution on time frames – let them know of the conditions that you've decided you want to put in your offer and if the time frames wouldn't put you under any unnecessary pressure.

Your offer will now have conditions favourable to the seller's circumstances, giving you the upper hand on other buyers even before price is discussed.

And you have the peace of mind that you will comfortably meet those conditions.

Try keep all other conditions to a minimum, but always ask for a building and pest inspection and finance clause if required.

Now, back to our example.

Understanding that the property is truly worth $620,000 - $630,000, and you haven't wasted any time along the way, you submit an offer of $590,000.

It's a strong offer, although you may decide to offer slightly less.

If your offer is accepted at this point, not only have you avoided overpaying, but you've picked up the property well under its true value. By acting quickly, tailoring your offer, and knowing the true value of the investment, you've saved yourself $30,000 - $40,000 upfront.

Now it's time for any professional inspections, namely the building and pest inspection which should always be requested.

And thanks to our earlier nibbling example, we may chip off another $6,000 from the deal.

Compare this scenario of saving $36,000 - $46,000 upfront, with buying a brand-new or off-the-plan development where the investor pays $100,000 above what the property is truly worth. That's a difference of $136,000 - $146,000 in savings from day one.

Not a bad result.

That's the benefit of the right guidance.

19

REAL-LIFE PROPERTY DEALS

You might have heard that the most money in real estate gets made in the deal.

It's partly true, but not gospel. Remember compound growth?

Exceptional deals are there to be found, but if you've cultivated a reliable and trustworthy reputation among the right people, these deals will find you.

And that's exactly what happened in this first example.

Example deal #1

I got a call from a property manager one day, notifying me that one of their landlords wanted to sell his property. He didn't want to go through the hassle of the sales process, marketing campaigns, professional photography, preparing for inspections, potentially wasting time and paying the agent commission.

A common story.

The market was booming, and no-one else knew about the property – so with a raised interest, we began the due diligence.

The property ticked the boxes:

- huge land component, even sub-dividable
- well-maintained house
- exceptional location near the train station, beach, shops
- short commute to Adelaide CBD
- chronically under-supplied market, fully developed with limited options for future building.

All other checks were also satisfactory, from the suburb, to the block, and the build itself.

What an opportunity.

My brother and I carried out a Comparative Market Analysis (checking nearby, recent sales) and determined that if the property were to go to market, it would sell for $560,000 - $570,000, based on the then current market conditions.

And the owner was asking low $500,000s.

If the owner had chosen to list their property through one of the best agents in the area, they likely would have achieved $560,000 - $570,000.

And that's the price of just one mistake.

The seller wanted a serious buyer, someone whose finance was lined up, allowing for a simple transaction to take place.

No frills, just a genuine offer.

And we had just the buyer.

We inspected the property and found several maintenance concerns, nothing detrimental, but there had to be some repairs made. We went ahead with an offer of $500,000 with very few conditions, just as the seller wanted. These simply included a twenty-one-day finance clause and a building and pest inspection.

The owner got back to us immediately asking for $510,000.

Absolutely thrilled, I held back my enthusiasm knowing that my client would certainly agree to a $10,000 increase.

And this is where most people would agree on the spot. A critical mistake in negotiating. But I remembered that in a negotiation like this, both parties tend to think they have less power than they actually have. Could I get them to agree to $500,000?

Using the higher authority gambit, I bought a little time and information. And from that phone call alone, I knew $500,000 was going to get us over the line.

I emailed the seller the list of maintenance concerns and for this reason my client's absolute maximum was $500,000. We had no intention of requesting a further discount after the building and pest inspection was completed, if only minor problems were found.

And it wasn't long until I got the call that our offer had been accepted.

Unfortunately, the owner deceitfully used a couch to hide a patch of water damage in one of the walls, not found until after settlement. This costed the client $5,000 to repair and quite a bit of stress.

We didn't have to, but we decided to waive our entire fee. And that's just life sometimes.

Several months later, comparable properties were now selling for over $600,000.

Example deal #2

This time we found a property on the open market but still managed to secure it far below its intrinsic value.

Prices were rising rapidly, and our suburb research suggested the market was still significantly undervalued.

I noticed a poorly-taken profile shot of a house in a suburb we were targeting. Opening the online ad, I immediately identified the lack of care and effort in putting the ad together.

The photos were blurry, the description short and vague. The selling agency were one of the smallest in the area, so I knew they would love to get a deal over the line.

Reading through the description, I noticed they preferred to sell to an investor because the owner didn't want the long-term tenant to have to find a new home. There were still several months left on the lease, and the tenant was paying significantly below-market rent.

This would keep many owner-occupiers away, along with many investors who would simply see a poor rental return. With such unappealing photos, many people might not have opened the ad at all.

Knowing that the rent was so low, and that investors make up the minority of buyer competition across Australia, I knew we could pick this property up at a great price.

The property was incredibly well located, and all the due diligence checks were carried out and satisfactory.

This is the kind of property we would consider to be investment-grade. We would expect a growth rate of 7.5% - 8.5% per annum over the long-term.

We carried out a Comparative Market Analysis and placed the true value at $510,000 - $520,000.

There was also scope for potential value-add work, which the client was looking for.

Little negotiating was involved. We simply tailored the conditions of our offer to exactly what the seller wanted and agreed to renegotiate a twelve-month lease to ensure the owner knew that we were willing to keep the tenant.

We paid under $475,000, which was approximately $40,000 less than if it were marketed successfully.

The rent was brought up to fair market level, the tenant could remain, and the seller had peace of mind knowing that the tenant wasn't going to be evicted at the expiry of the lease.

Getting the best deal isn't about low-balling and hoping for the best. It's about finding or creating a situation where all parties involved get a positive outcome.

You don't want to miss out on dozens of properties and drag the search out for months. The market may rise fifty thousand dollars in that time. By initially offering a more reasonable price, this extra growth could've been a part of your portfolio.

Not to mention a low-ball offer might put the seller off and not consider you a serious buyer.

The traditional mindset of buyer versus seller needs to be changed. It subconsciously infers that only one will win at the negotiating table, when the best deals of the day are win-win scenarios.

If you decide to buy in a hot market and have had no luck with finding these unique scenarios to buy under-market-value, then a fair offer to secure the right property is entirely reasonable. As we have seen, the property will be investment-grade, greatly outperform the rest of the market, and get you one step further to completing your portfolio.

One final note for getting the best deal; regardless of any hiccups or setbacks along the way, always remain emotionally controlled. If you leave a negative impact on the agent by reacting poorly, then you aren't likely to be at the top of their list when future opportunities arise.

I do empathise with the fact that some days agents have to make twenty calls to buyers who missed out on a property and only one call of congratulations. Perhaps that's naïve.

It can be difficult, as the buying process can be a highly emotional time. And missing out on a great property that you thought was 'the one' can be hugely disappointing.

To sum up:

- Find out what the seller wants out of the transaction other than the highest sale price.
- Provide reasoning if you submit a lower offer.
- Tailor your conditions as much as possible to suit the seller.
- Give confidence that your finance is arranged.
- Control any negative emotions or reactions at all times.

20

THE UNFAIR POWER OF MENTORSHIP

It's common to want to beat the market on your own, to be completely self-made. You've built your empire from the ground-up, with your own blood, sweat, and tears. I'm with you! I was the same when I started out on my journey.

But what if we leave our egos right here (insert ego) and come back to it later?

Now, take five seconds, and take a deep breath.

Imagine you've been actively investing in property for over a decade. You've bought and sold many of your own properties, all over the country, both residential and commercial.

You've bought and held properties with a capital growth focus, cash flow focus, and properties with a healthy combination of the two.

You've bought both new and established properties.

You've renovated some, and you've completely set-and-forget others.

You've bought in many different structures, and you've even managed your own properties from time to time.

You've experienced market booms and busts, bought and held properties during both of these economic conditions.

Now ask yourself: did you make any mistakes along the way?

Did you learn any lessons?

Hopefully you would have only made half a dozen mistakes or less, with no detriment to your portfolio. With about five per cent of properties on the market what we would consider 'investment-grade' at any given time, hopefully these properties were the ones that you bought, and at the lowest possible price.

Would you tell your younger self how to avoid the minefield of traps out there, who to listen to and who to ignore, and what type of properties significantly outperformed the rest over that period?

Or would there be nothing to gain from such advice?

Thousands of mistakes can be made in property investment, and education will only get you so far in negating them. Education can allow you to beat the crowd and massively amplify your results.

But experience is the ultimate teacher.

The right mentor can help you get to the next level, the level beyond self-education.

And a single mistake could set you back more in cost than a decade of professional help.

Cultivating a relationship with the right mentor will make this journey faster, safer, and significantly more rewarding.

And that's exactly why JSC Property Investments was founded. Bringing authenticity, extensive experience, and a passion for property - without the exorbitant price tag.

I never had a mentor, but as a twenty-year-old full of drive and self-motivation, I believed I could read and research endlessly, until I learned all the strategies of the most successful property investors.

Many books contradicted each other, some promoting cash flow properties, others promoting capital growth properties. Some promoted extremely high-risk investing.

It wasn't until after I had bought several properties that I found out a lot of these strategies aren't relevant in today's property market. Many strategies that were effective pre-GFC (2008) just aren't suitable for the property market of today. Lending requirements have changed, buying and selling costs have increased, affordability and rental yields have changed, and the process of applying for a loan is more in-depth and time-consuming.

This means that some strategies need to be altered or ignored altogether.

And it must be said that the books promoting these outdated strategies are not nearly as effective as they once were.

But how would an inexperienced investor know which strategies to avoid and which strategies are effective? The authors seem reputable, genuine, and they have clearly been in the industry for a long time.

This is where the right mentor becomes extremely valuable.

Bring your freedom years closer, bring more flexibility and choices into your life.

And get a mentor.

21

WHERE TO FROM HERE?

If you've read this far, I thank you for the time you've committed to this book. I'm not a professional writer, nor am I a salesman with contagious, charismatic energy.

I wouldn't know how to sell you this pen.

But I do put integrity before personal gain and the health and wellbeing of others before self-vested profits. As a result, I've chosen to use my knowledge and experience for the greater benefit of others and turn down any huge commissions offered to push certain properties onto clients.

You might be excited to begin or expand your property portfolio, and you've probably thought about how much passive income or capital growth you would like your properties to achieve to reach your goals.

Now it's time to talk to a great mortgage broker or your preferred mortgage lending institution to discuss your options. This should give you some insight into your budget for your next property, or tips and advice on how to get in a position to get a loan and grow the portfolio.

If you feel confident enough to navigate the property investing game on your own, then I hope you do exceptionally well. Feel free to check out our YouTube channel, Podcasts, Instagram, Facebook, and LinkedIn for free educational material that might assist you along the way.

But if you'd prefer some support and guidance, if you aren't sure about where or what to buy, or maybe you simply don't have the time to buy a property, then a buyer's agent might be the right choice for you.

Did you hear that? Sounded like the rustle of spruikers' ears popping up. As a final note, if you do decide to choose a professional buyer's agent for your next purchase, do your future, wealthier self a massive favour and make sure they genuinely have your best interests at the core of what they do.

How do you know?

- A buyer's agent should work exclusively for the buyer, without hidden commissions or agendas to push any specific property.
- A buyer's agent or sourcing specialist recommending brand-new builds is

potentially receiving huge commissions from the sale, that you will pay for in its entirety. Speculation of huge profits upon completion are just that – speculation. Don't forget to inquire about the size of the blocks for these new properties.

- Check online reviews through Google or social media. Look at older reviews if available to see how they started out.
- A buyer's agent might think they know what makes a great investment, but if they don't have their own vast amounts of personal and professional experience in property investing, then mistakes can still be made, and the buyer bears the cost.
- Never forget to ask if the buyer's agent has a real estate license. This ensures some level of legitimacy and baseline knowledge of real estate. Many companies today are flying under-the-radar and get away without having a license because of particular loopholes in current legislation.

What can you expect if you want to work with JSC Property Investments?

1 **Tell us your goals**

We'll work with you to clarify your property investment goals based on your current situation and where you would like to be.

2 **Create a strategy to maximise your future portfolio**

We will create a tailored plan most suitable to your situation, including target locations and specific property criteria to suit your goals.

3 **Finance pre-approval**

We'll put you in touch with an outstanding, investor-savvy mortgage broker who understands how an investor's finance needs to be arranged to create a multi-property portfolio. They will ensure there is no lending roadblocks along the way – which can be detrimental to a high-performing portfolio!

4 **Property acquisition**

We begin the search for all on- and off-market properties, utilising our existing networks for the most up-to-date listings and properties that never hit the open market. Once a property that matches your criteria is found, exhaustive due diligence and inspections are conducted, and we begin the negotiating to get the best possible price.

5 **Ongoing property management**

We'll put you in touch with the best property management company in the area, ensuring your property is always occupied, well-cared for, and providing maximum cash flow with the best possible rental return. They will also conduct regular rent reviews ensuring your property is always performing as strongly as possible.

6 **Annual reviews**

The team at JSC conduct annual reviews (at a minimum) to ensure that your portfolio continues to outperform, and to plan ahead for future purchases to complete the portfolio.

Simply send us an email at
info@jscpropertyinvestments.com.au

As we have seen, few investors ever create significant wealth through property. There are too many traps, too many big-budget companies clogging up the scroll feed ads with execrable new builds that aren't good for investors.

There's a tremendous lack of genuine guidance and support available, leading countless investors to stagnate at only one or two properties or abandon their journey altogether.

And investors just can't afford to learn through trial and error. Invest wisely, and you'll realise just how profitable property investing can truly be.

There's a reason why you've turned to property investment. There's a reason why you're reading this book. There's a goal you want to achieve or a change that you want to make.

Stick with the guidance and principles in this book, and that goal can be achieved. No gimmicks, no sales pitch, no ulterior motives.

Just a dream to improve the quality of life through successful property investment.

Happy investing,

Jacob

REFERENCES

Page 56 on land tax

- https://www.revenuesa.sa.gov.au/landtax/calculate-land-tax/2022-23-general-land-tax-rates-calculator
- https://qro.qld.gov.au/land-tax/calculate/individual/
- https://www.apps09.revenue.nsw.gov.au/erevenue/calculators/landtax.php
- https://www.revenue.act.gov.au/land-tax?result_1060955_result_page=2
- https://www.sro.vic.gov.au/land-tax-current-rates
- https://www.sro.tas.gov.au/land-tax/land-tax-calculator
- https://www.wa.gov.au/organisation/department-of-finance/land-tax-assessment

Page 95 – 'Bricks and slaughter' news article

- https://www.youtube.com/watch?v=smPR0s2W-Ck&ab_channel=60MinutesAustralia

News segment on 60 minutes
Reporter: Tom Steinfort
16th September 2018

Page 95 – Housing Debt Stress

- https://www.abc.net.au/news/2022-05-02/borrowers-home-loans-mortgage-stress-interest-rate-rise-election/101026362

ABC News
Reporter: Nassim Khadem
2nd May 2022